Bulls, Bears,
and
Millionaires
War Stories of the
Trading Life

Robert Koppel

Dearborn
Financial Publishing, Inc.®

This publication is designed to provide accurate and authoritative information in regard to the subject matter covered. It is sold with the understanding that the publisher is not engaged in rendering legal, accounting, or other professional service. If legal advice or other expert assistance is required, the services of a competent professional person should be sought.

Executive Editor: Cynthia A. Zigmund
Managing Editor: Jack Kiburz
Interior Design: Lucy Jenkins
Cover Design: Scott Rattray, Rattray Design
Typesetting: Elizabeth Pitts

97 98 99 10 9 8 7 6 5 4 3 2

Library of Congress Cataloging-in-Publication Data

Koppel, Robert.
    Bulls, bears, and millionaires : war stories of the trading life /
Robert Koppel.
        p.   cm.
    Includes index.
    ISBN 0-7931-2393-3 (hardcover)
    1. Stockbrokers—United States—Case studies. 2. Stockbrokers—
Psychology. 3. Success in business.   I. Title.
HG4621.K66   1997
332.64′092′273—dc21   97-6381
                                                              CIP

Dearborn books are available at special quantity discounts to use as premiums and sales promotions, or for use in corporate training programs. For more information, please call the Special Sales Manager at 800-621-9621, ext. 4384, or write to Dearborn Financial Publishing, Inc., 155 N. Wacker Drive, Chicago, IL 60606-1719.

Dedication

To my family
Mara, Lily, and Niko

Praise for *Bulls, Bears, and Millionaires*

"*Bulls, Bears, and Millionaires* offers the reader tremendous perspective on the psychological makeup of winning traders through their life stories. I learned an awful lot from reading this book."

—Toby Crabel, President
Crabel Capital Management

"In *Bulls, Bears, and Millionaires* Bob Koppel brings us a fascinating look at the hearts and minds of top performing traders. No serious trader or investor should miss this book."

—Lawrence Rosenberg, Former Chairman
Chicago Mercantile Exchange, and Member,
Chicago Board of Trade

"The people described in *Bulls, Bears, and Millionaires* inhabit a ruthless realm where millions of dollars can change hands in a matter of minutes. This book is about how they got where they are and what makes them tick. If you're a trader or contemplating becoming one, you'll enjoy these insights into the trading persona."

—A. Thomas Shanks, President
Hawksbill Capital Management

"*Bulls, Bears, and Millionaires* is truly the 'inside stuff.' You'll learn why the best and brightest love to trade and how they constantly sharpen their competitive edge."

—Angelo Reynolds, Member
International Monetary Market

"*Bulls, Bears, and Millionaires* is a delightful collection of 'tell-all' tales from some of the world's most gifted traders and analysts, and Bob Koppel brings these characters vividly to life. The reader is allowed to delve into the minds of these professional traders and learn the very elements of their success. It is truly fun and fascinating reading."

—Robin Mesch, Chief Fixed-Income Analyst
Thomson Research

"No one else could have produced a book of such central importance to traders with so much insight, charm, and wit."

—Howard Abell, Author
The Day Traders Advantage

"For those interested in the trial by fire world of trading, Bob Koppel offers a nonflammable and entertaining way to gain surefire insights in *Bulls, Bears, and Millionaires*."

—Tim McAuliffe, Member
International Monetary Market

"A penetrating look at the lives of traders, the reader experiences the world of financial warriors fighting courageously on the battlefield of everyday life."

—Steve Moore, President
Moore Research Center, Inc.

"Terrific insight into the trading world. A must read, no matter what your personal level of trading or investing."

—Larry Carr, Member
Chicago Board of Trade

"Bob Koppel combines scholarship with firsthand knowledge in this exciting and rare perspective of the high stakes psychological risks and rewards of the trading life."

—Kevin McAuliffe
Rand Financial Services, Inc.

"*Bulls, Bears, and Millionaires* is a unique look at the trading theater. The 'war stories' presented range from humorous to tragic to insightful and inspirational."

—Marshall Stein, Director
Chicago Mercantile Exchange

"What's the key to making it as a trader? Ultimately, the trader must refuse to be anything else but a trader. That's the lesson to be gleaned from Koppel's *Bulls, Bears, and Millionaires*. Real tales from real traders that walk you through their personal stories, living through the low points to find success on the other side."

—Thomas Hartle, Editor
Technical Analysis of Stocks and Commodities

"An interviewer who understands the meaning of an attitude . . . Koppel, who is also a knowledgeable trader, is very adept in *Bulls, Bears, and Millionaires* at extracting the best ideas from other successful traders! The end result . . . How can the author and interviewee best articulate the intangible attitude and focused direction of a good trader's methods of winning at trading? New traders by inference will be able to understand themselves better and define accurately what they wish their own trading framework to be . . . particularly their mental attitude."

—Tim Slater, Managing Director
Dow Jones Telerate, Inc.

"The fascinating stories in *Bulls, Bears, and Millionaires* reveal what it takes to succeed at business and in life. The golden thread that is the core of these diverse and distinctive traders is incredible persistence; willingness to learn from a harsh taskmaster—the market itself; the ability to submerge their egos; learning from mistakes; accepting responsibilities for their decisions; and being disciplined about keeping their perspective in the midst of two very powerful human traits—greed and fear. If you are serious about investing, I highly recommend this book for insight into the character, resilience and risk tolerance required to keep your head while all others around you are losing theirs."

—Linda Chandler, Former Senior Vice President,
Sutro & Co., and Author of *Winning Strategies
for Capital Formation*

CONTENTS

Foreword   viii
Preface   x
Acknowledgments   xi
Introduction   xii

1. A Personal Tale   1
2. Chairman Jack *Jack Sandner*   8
3. Rocket Man *Mike Dever*   16
4. Solomon's Mind *Solomon Cohen*   33
5. Fly on a Rhino's Back *Timothy McAuliffe*   47
6. Trading Suits Him *Larry Rosenberg*   56
7. Tennis Anyone? *William H. "Toby" Crabel*   68
8. Hook, Line, and Sinker *Dennis Weinmann*   75
9. Seeing Is Believing *David M. Gordon*   87
10. A View from the Bridge *Marshall Stein*   96
11. Trades to the Beat of Her Own Drummond
    Robin Mesch   106
12. Is There an Austrian Magician in the House?
    Scott A. Foster   116
13. Learn to Learn *A. Thomas Shanks*   129
14. Lady Luck *Arlene Busch*   139
15. The Comeback Kid *Jerry Letterman*   149
16. West of Eden *David Lansburgh*   157
17. Tom's Edge *Tom Grossman*   167
18. Hard Times and Losin' It *Bryan Gindoff*   179
19. Momma Said There'd Be Days Like This
    Angelo Reynolds   188
20. Futures and Options   198

Index   204
About the Author   209

FOREWORD

Wives are rarely invited to write forewords to their husbands' books. I am in a unique position to take on this task. Most of our 20 years together have been played out against the psychologically and physically demanding life of trading. Some of that time has seemed like an enchanted vacation on a luxury yacht. But there also have been periods when it seemed we were bailing water out of a leaky rowboat and fending off rocks, while fighting for our financial and emotional survival. I've been through it all with Bob, who has continued to be a miner of insights, a "mapmaker" for others in one of the most treacherous and rewarding occupations imaginable. His own real-life experiences and continuing intellectual fascination with the market make it possible for him to lead the reader into the trading arena with a memorable selection of traders who reflect on their past battles, and the preparation, battle strategies, wounds induced or received, the strength gained from new learning, returning again and again to the fray.

I have known Bob as a bull, a bear, and a millionaire with all the intervening stages. As these remarkable interviews reveal, there is no quick transformation of a fledgling trader into a battler of bulls, a baiter of bears, or even a millionaire. It is a constant tempering process that takes everything you've got and can turn that Armani suit back into a pair of jeans in a tick. This book probes the personalities, styles, and human qualities that make these consummate players uniquely adapted to maneuver in a volcano-like tumult. It is an ongoing learning experience forged with skill, courage, and humility, a human drama of Shakespearean breadth. Like Chaucer's pilgrims, no two are alike but all are bound by a common undertaking. Their backgrounds and paths to their occupations are as varied and surprising as the markets they trade as floor traders or managers of hedge-fund billions with a brain surgeon's precision combined with a bulldog's tenacity. "Rocket Man" brings a lifelong interest in astronomy to gazing at the stars and black holes of the markets. A magician's skill with sleight-of-hand is revealed in another's trading performance. Sports are well represented across the board: an all-American tennis player who still believes practice delivers the winner, a racquetball pro, a final-four basketball star, and the Golden Gloves boxer/professional dancer who ultimately combined force and grace as chairman of one of the world's leading financial exchanges. Academics and the arts are represented as well, as seen in the mathematician/musician who spends time on the piano bench with Beethoven sonatas.

These ordinary and, at the same time, extraordinary men and women who recount their ongoing voyages of self-discovery come from all walks of social and economic life. One, with an Italian first name, is the only African-American trading in the hive-like Eurodollar pit. These stories ring with their own personal hard-won truths about the drives and struggles that go on beneath the inadequate armor of the trading jacket. They will inspire the reader with their tellers' tested belief in themselves and their ability to succeed at one of the toughest games going.

—Mara Koppel

PREFACE

The trading floors on the world's financial exchanges are a human comedy of high drama and low pratfall. They are a self-contained, at times incomprehensible, world of arcane expressions and aggressive physical money signals. To the outsider it is an alien, indecipherable megabuck realm of pulsating bodies and fever-pitched shouting where emotions and lifestyles are as volatile as fast-ticking price changes. It is a world of speed and reactions fueled by fear and greed often based on superstition, neurosis, and a need for extravagant and high-risk living.

A collective psychology is at work in this world, where it has been said there are more millionaires per square inch than anywhere else on Earth: a roaring, breathless passion to make money, to let profits pile up like pleasing snowdrifts, and to stay one step ahead of the competition, where the difference between success and failure is measured in nanoseconds.

Through a series of interviews and never-before-told "war stories," the reader is invited to experience the inner workings of this fascinating, little-known world of shadowy and enlightened speculators and money managers who are on the front lines of an open-outcry system based on brains, guts, and timing.

I believe *Bulls, Bears, and Millionaires* is unique in its inside frontline coverage of the trading theater, where I have been a player for 18 years as well as a colleague of many of the industry's most important figures. I truly feel humble to be able to write about an industry that I have grown to know and appreciate for its subtle comedy and complexity.

It is in this spirit that I ask the reader to consider *Bulls, Bears, and Millionaires* as a compelling human drama about trading campaigns and psychological battles, hard fought and sometimes won. I believe the stories are riveting lessons for all of us about emotional volatility, risk taking, courage, discipline, and survival, and an often ironic look at the internal warfare that rages within us all to achieve victory on the battlefield of personal success.

ACKNOWLEDGMENTS

I wish to thank all the traders who generously shared with me their ideas and frontline trading experiences. They are: Arlene Busch, Solomon Cohen, William H. "Toby" Crabel, Mike Dever, Scott A. Foster, Bryan Gindoff, David Gordon, Tom Grossman, David Lansburgh, Jerry Letterman, Robin Mesch, Tim McAuliffe, Angelo Reynolds, Larry Rosenberg, Jack Sandner, A. Thomas Shanks, Marshall Stein, and Dennis Weinmann.

In particular, I wish to thank my friend and business partner Howard Abell for being just the person he is, although apologetically, all too often I chide him for his "cynical" (a.k.a. faultlessly accurate) perceptions of events and individuals. Thanks also goes to Mara Koppel whose intellectual rigor and strong character have served as both an example and inspiration.

This book is not a work of fiction. The names, characters, and events portrayed are not the product of an author's imagination. Any resemblance to real events or actual persons living or dead is entirely uncoincidental. It is to my readers that I owe the ultimate acknowledgment for continually reminding me of this fact in their kind letters and conversations; they make all my work worthwhile.

INTRODUCTION

In the late 1980s, an award-winning journalist named Richard Ben Cramer began bird-dogging six White House contenders in order to shed light on a fascinating and perplexing question that surely must be as old as our republic: "How do presumably ordinary people acquire that mixture of ambition, stamina, and pure shamelessness that makes a true candidate?" When *What It Takes,* the fruit of Cramer's labors, was published in 1992, it garnered near-universal praise and acclaim, along with "Book of the Year" honors from *Time.*

In similar manner, Robert Koppel lately has set out to get to the bottom of a series of even older questions—questions about traders and trading that are as fundamental and ancient as civilization's earliest bazaars. Why, for example, do men and women choose to become traders? Are the best traders born or made? Are they infallible, invincible, and/or invulnerable? Is there a foolproof formula for success in trading? The answers to these and many other questions can be found right here in *Bulls, Bears, and*

Millionaires: War Stories of the Trading Life, which is Bob Koppel's "What It Takes."

Early on in this volume, Koppel refers to the trading floor of the Chicago Mercantile Exchange (CME) as a "closed information shop." As he puts it, when he first ventured into the pits, "there was an unwritten code on the exchange that traders didn't give or seek advice. . . ." Heedless of, or oblivious to, such structures, the precocious author-to-be proceeded to make it a point to speak each and every day to the CME's elite traders—the "titans," as he terms them—for clues on how he could hone his trading skills. Twenty years and four books later, Koppel still has the knack. While his universe has expanded considerably, he still knows a titan when he sees one, whether in Chicago, New York, London, or anywhere else. And he continues to this day to ask exactly the questions that will prompt these elite traders to open up in surprising ways about what they do, why they do it, and exactly how they go about it.

Yes, Koppel has been down this path before. With coauthor, friend, and business partner Howard Abell, he penned *The Inner-game of Trading* (Irwin, 1993) and *The Outer Game of Trading* (Irwin, 1994). His first solo effort, *The Intuitive Trader* (Wiley), was released last year. This time around, he breaks fresh ground as 19 traders, among them the author himself, relate their personal stories in the form of answers to his perceptive queries.

The *crème de la crème* Koppel has assembled this time is as varied as are modern financial markets. There are floor traders, "upstairs" traders, fund managers, and even a manager of 50 other traders, herself a onetime options trader. Some trade securities, some trade futures, some trade options, some trade them all. These distinctions aside, in telling respects they are strikingly the same. Whether they have earned advanced degrees or high-school diplomas, all are smart, alert, and very much open to new thinking and fresh ideas. Most have a facility for logic, mathematics, and problem solving, and at least two are accomplished musicians. Almost all have played sports of one kind or another and most have excelled. Indeed, they are competitive enough to have won championships in boxing, basketball, racquetball, tennis, and even ballroom dancing.

More than anything else, this is a book about adversity and failure and, ultimately, redemption. At one time or another, virtually every one of these bulls, bears, and millionaires has failed, often in truly spectacular fashion. While some of their stories are downright harrowing and a few lost just about everything, these traders never for a moment quit, never even considered retreating to the sidelines to join the hanger-on "like aged prize fighters past their prime," as Koppel sees them, "content to relive in their own minds former moments of glory."

This is fascinating reading for anyone who aspires to invest in, write about, or trade in financial markets. In essence, these interviews amount to a series of insightful, refreshing, and often irreverent first-person accounts of one of the most innovative, turbulent, and exciting periods in the history of modern finance.

—T. Eric "Rick" Kilcollin
President and CEO
Chicago Mercantile Exchange

CHAPTER 1

A Personal Tale

Life shrinks or expands in proportion to one's courage.
—Anaïs Nin

In 1976, I moved to Chicago filled with an amorphous ambition to "make it big." Before that my artist wife and I had lived in a small village in the Berkshires, where we were writing film scripts that were magnets for rejection notices. Our life together was a situation comedy of art, literature, and grousing about not having enough money. Two years earlier, my younger brother had moved to Chicago where he was working in the financial district as a commodities broker. A meteoric rise in the pork belly market transformed him overnight into a millionaire.

Alan, a no-nonsense, bottom-line kind of guy soon after invited me, all expenses paid, to witness his dramatic lifestyle change. A year earlier he had lived in a one-bedroom apartment next to the El tracks; when I visited him he was ensconced in the Loire Valley style of Highland Park, one of Chicago's ritzier suburbs. In the *de rigueur* North Shore manner, the house featured a swimming pool, tennis court, and a garage stocked with luxury automobiles. Of course there was also a beautiful wife who loved to shop and an adoring and attentive staff representing all continents with the exception of Antarctica. On a lark, at his request, I spent a day with him at work, observing his operations on the trading floor.

My first impression was that the floor resembled the Great Barrier Reef, a virtual kaleidoscopic swell of activity with traders, exchange employees, and runners, color-coded in aggressive neon shades, scurrying about with all the single-mindedness of sperm cells; a teeming, self-contained sexual environment where only the most well-adapted life forms survive.

The mid-70s was the heyday of the Chicago markets. Even a First Lady could make a killing! The mood was encapsulated in the corporate motto of the clearing firm owned by the chairman of the Chicago Mercantile Exchange. "Free markets for free men." The atmosphere on the trading floor was high voltage, direct current. Each tick change on the price board transmitted the feeling of running a brand new Porsche Targa through its gears.

As a trader, each moment was like the deciding game of a seven-game World Series: bases loaded, bottom of the ninth, three-and-two count. You literally could feel the intensity and charge right down to the soles of your shoes. You could smell the piquant aroma of money like freshly brewed coffee in the air.

The other initial impression that stands out is the special camaraderie that existed among the traders. They had gashouse gang–like nicknames for each other: "Cadillac Jack," "Spit-shine," "Slim" who weighed about 450 pounds, "the Count," and "Pickle Man," a guy from the southwest side of Chicago who had made a fortune in the Polish pickle business and was in the process of making another in the cattle and hog markets. He looked like Attila the Hun sporting a Rolex watch and Luchese boots.

Three months later, my wife and I moved to Chicago. I was hooked. I felt the lure and wonder of this Runyonesque world. I was ready, willing, and unable.

In those days, it was relatively inexpensive to get started in trading. My brother lent me $10,000, which I was instructed was not only to be used for speculative capital but was meant to cover living expenses for the entire year. At first I found trading in the pit very difficult. It took three months before I had my first winning day. Six months into it I lost everything and Alan informed me in a rare moment of pique that I was a complete "screw-up," he'd have no part of it, and I should consider myself to be on my own!

Motivation is a key factor in trading and my brother's revelation certainly was a strong incentive for me to turn things around. I arranged with the president of the clearing firm that I was doing business with to allow me to continue trading as long as I didn't run a debit account. I started trading more actively than I had in the preceding months and began to pay close attention to what the best traders on the floor were doing. I made it a point each day to speak to the elite traders, who were accorded titan-like status, to find out what I needed to do to improve. This sounds pretty tame now, but in 1976 there was an unwritten code on the exchange that traders didn't give or seek advice from other members. In those days, the trading floor was a closed-information shop.

At first I was trading only one or two contracts (which are like shares of stock) but within a relatively short period of time I was moving hundreds and within a couple of years holding limit positions—the largest position size allowable by federal law. In short, I was now becoming a player. I was good and I knew it—and so did everyone else.

At 40, I had made millions in the market and felt invulnerable, a not-uncommon, although lethal, feeling among traders. In my mind I was the prince of the city, the king of the mountain. I was like that old guy who lived on Mount St. Helens before the volcano erupted. He too refused to move off his mountain, believing unquestionably that it wouldn't blow. Of course the scientists and experts are always wrong!

The funny thing is that when my mountain blew, a ten on my Richter scale, it didn't result from a loss in the markets. I was too smart to lose money that way! That was for the suckers who, lacking discipline and personal character, would allow themselves to become emotionally attached to losing positions like salami attaching itself to the slicer. My downfall, on the other hand, was dictated by accepting bad advice from accountants and money managers and from a neurotic addiction to imperial living. I'll spare the details, but think the biggest, best, and most expensive, and I lived in it, wore it, drove it, vacationed there, and ate it. My grandfather was right: Everything we truly learn or understand in life creates in us a deeper sense of our own humility. At 42, I was definitely humbled.

I lost everything material that I had worked for. In addition, I found myself deeply in debt. I believed I had no chance of ever recovering; my situation seemed hopeless. I was worse than broke—I had to earn a fortune just to get to broke!

As you can imagine, this placed an unbelievable strain on my family. In a very short time we went from chateaubriand to château Spam. The legion of sycophants and hangers-on who routinely called at our door was gone, as were the invitations to dinners, parties, gallery openings, and charity events. We felt spurned, isolated, and abandoned by many from whom we expected more. My wife sold her wedding ring to secure a deposit on our rented apartment. Happily, all this is behind us now. But I also must add: it is and it isn't.

This is of course a personal story, but in many ways it is not a unique story. Until quite recently I was a principal of a member clearing firm on the world's largest exchange. One of the traders I hired was in the early 80s one of the most influential commodity traders in the country with an estimated personal net worth exceeding a hundred million dollars. When I interviewed James, a likable, down-to-earth guy in his late forties with Al Pacino looks, he told me that he had lost everything and all he needed was one more chance. I gave it to him but it didn't work out. The market had taken its psychological toll on him.

There are many like James who, having once tasted the excitement and frenzy of trading success, search with an obsessive compulsion for the next electrical jolt; for them, unfortunately, the keys to the treasure chest are forever lost. They are the burned-out traders who hang out on the periphery of the trading pits and board rooms; like aged prize fighters past their prime, they relive in their own minds former moments of glory. They are bruised knights endlessly battling internal windmills.

Others, like Patrick Arbor, the current chairman of the Chicago Board of Trade, refused to give up. Earlier in his career, after a series of reckless losses, Arbor suffered the ultimate shame for a trader, "busting out." At 6 feet 1 inch, with the lean, taut build of a long-distance runner, Arbor spent 18 months welding I beams 45 stories above LaSalle Street on one of Chicago's Loop skyscrapers in order to put a stake together to get back to trading. It was from this Olympian vantage point that he discovered strengths within himself that he did not know existed and vowed never again to be brought down so low. He concluded that what took him down was a volatile mix of emotion and greed. What he needed to learn was, in a word, discipline. As a youngster growing up in an alcoholic family, Arbor seemed more destined for a life on the street than in the executive office of the Chicago Board of Trade. Arbor placed himself on a daily regimen. He didn't smoke or drink alcohol or even caffeine. He developed personal rules about the way he walked, talked, ate, and stood. He would put himself through a series of daily rituals such as standing on his toes for extended periods of time just to see how much pain he could endure as a means of achieving self-control.

It is fascinating to explore the backgrounds and influences that produced these contemporary Horatio Algers who fight tooth and nail, no matter what, to secure their goals. Tough, scrappy, disciplined soldiers fighting daily all in the name of capitalistic hope and financial survival.

Jack Sandner was a former top-notch amateur boxer. A Golden Gloves winner, he had an impressive 58-and-2 record. At 5 feet 4 inches and with a Peter-Pan face and strawberry-gray hair, Sandner is a wiry and fast-moving featherweight, except when it comes to trading and the global financial markets, where by anyone's standards he's decidedly a superheavyweight. The twists and turns in Sandner's life are truly remarkable: street kid, gas station attendant, prize fighter, high-school dropout, class valedictorian, professional dancer, Las Vegas blackjack dealer, law review editor, and chairman of the board of the Chicago Mercantile Exchange and the International Monetary Market.

Coincidentally, Sandner and Arbor, in addition to directing the world's two largest financial exchanges and having similar trading experiences of near financial ruin, share something else in common. Forty-five years earlier, both resided on Chicago's tough West Side and found inspiration from a young priest, Father Kelly, at Mercy Home for Boys. Only in America!

Leo Melamed, generally considered the father of financial futures, understands better than anyone the importance and irony of his personal history on the development of the global market. Born in 1932, Melamed too is a survivor. With his family, Leo fled Russian pogroms and the German blitzkrieg. In fear for their lives, the Melameds traveled by train across Siberia to Vladivostok and from there went on to Japan. Eventually, the family settled on Chicago's Northwest Side, where Leo's father was a Yiddish teacher in a Hebrew school. His life story is a Dr. Zhivago–like epic of cunning, intelligence, perseverance, and personal discipline. Dark-skinned and diminutive with pug-like facial features that remind one of Edward G. Robinson, Melamed is still seen by many as the major power behind the throne of the international financial markets.

From the trading floor to the trading rooms and into the executive offices of the world's financial exchanges, there is a compelling psychology and attitude that stands out: to identify and implement what works without excuse or explanation, fearlessly embracing risk, and knowing there is no ultimate control or certainty.

The trading world is a high-wire act of talented performers who possess a thick-skinned aggressiveness and a fully focused, clear-eyed will to survive. Linda Leventhal, arguably the most successful female trader on the International Monetary Market, overcame family pressure, male chauvinism, a spastic colon, and a bad marriage to prove to herself and everyone else that she had what it takes. A former elementary school teacher with no prior experience in trading or investing, she set out to conquer the interest rate markets. Beginning small, she steadily piled up her winnings. When I interviewed her for *The Intuitive Trader* she informed me that her worst year out of a 15-year trading career was middle six figures.

The winners find ever-new and inventive ways to win. They scramble, scratch, and slug, all in the name of free enterprise and mounting profits. They know well their enemies: emotion, remorse, panic, fear, greed, and resentment. Their role is to constantly seize the advantage and to get the edge, whether it is a single pork belly futures contract or capturing market share of an international financial market. These men and women speculate not on markets or prices, chart patterns, or commodities, but in a literal sense on themselves. Day in and day out they confidently wager on their own ability to succeed, to survive, and to overcome all adversity that is placed in their way. They are the warriors and these are their stories.

"And the end of all our exploring
Will be to arrive where we started
And know the place for the first time."

—T.S. Eliot, *Little Gidding*

CHAPTER 2

Chairman Jack

Jack Sandner

Mr. Sandner, formerly a trial attorney, joined the Chicago Mercantile Exchange in 1971 and has served continuously on its governing board since 1977. He has served on and chaired many member committees. In 1978 he became president and CEO of RB&H, Inc., a futures commission merchant and clearing firm of the CME. First elected CME chairman in 1980, Mr. Sandner remained chairman for three consecutive terms through 1982, after which he served three years as board-appointed legislative liaison. He was elected chairman again in 1986 and re-elected for two more terms through 1988. In 1989 and 1990, he served as senior policy adviser before being elected chairman once again in 1991. He has served as chairman continuously through the 1991 election.

Q: Jack, you are chairman of the Chicago Mercantile Exchange, a position in which you have now served with distinction, for over 15 years. You also have many other fine accomplishments, but I feel compelled to ask you a question: I read somewhere that in your youth you were a professional disco dancer. Is there any truth to that?

Jack: I can assure you there's no truth to any stories about disco dancing. However, I did win the Harvest Moon Festival Dance Contest at the Chicago Stadium when I was 15 years old. Unfortunately, I think people confuse that with disco.

Q: What was the Harvest Moon Festival Dance contest?

Jack: It was one of the biggest dance contests in the country.

Q: Ballroom dancing?

Jack: Yes. I did rock-and-roll in high school, but this was ballroom. Every year there was a sellout crowd at the Chicago Stadium in November. It took a lot of work to get to there. You had to go through a series of dance contests for nine months at different high-school gyms all around the city. The actual night of the Harvest Moon Festival was a star-studded extravaganza.

The night that I won, Jayne Mansfield, Zsa Zsa Gabor, Charlton Heston, and James Arness were there. Jerry Lewis was the emcee. Archie Moore, who was fighting Floyd Patterson two weeks later in the stadium, was also there. Louie Armstrong was there! It was a big night to a sold-out crowd at the Chicago Stadium and I won, at the age of 15, so that's my dancing experience!

Q: Jack, you were also a Golden Gloves boxer. It's unusual, don't you think, for somebody to box and also to excel at dancing?

Jack: No! Quite the opposite. I tap danced right next to Sugar Ray Robinson at 63rd and Woodlawn at Theresa Dolan Dance Studios. There was a great boxing gym where I used to train, called Johnny Coolan's at 63rd and Dorchester. Two blocks away was this dance studio above the El tracks. Sugar Ray Robinson took tap lessons there whenever he was in Chicago for a fight. I went over there one day and put on tap shoes. Sugar Ray and I danced together, and that's how I learned how to tap dance! With great fighters it's all footwork. Look at Muhammad Ali; look at Sugar Ray Leonard. They all move great with their feet. Your feet take you places, quickly!

Q: Of all your many interests and achievements at an early age, which do you think prepared you best for a career in trading?

Jack: I think you'd have to go back to the recesses of the mind, what makes someone competitive, and what makes someone want to win. You learn that the desire to win and the ability to try to figure a way to win in whatever venue you're involved complement one another. For example, if it's boxing, the desire to win may translate into training very, very hard, working on different skill sets rather than just going in and being a brawler. You'll find a way to win, and usually it's through hard work and discipline rather than through luck and brute force. Obviously, you see that a lot in athletics. In the Harvest Moon Festival I wanted to win and I found a way to win, and it was through figuring out different dance steps with my partner that would be very appealing to the 11 judges. In boxing, if you're fighting a certain kind of a fighter, you'll fight a little differently. Is he a strong puncher or a stick-and-move–type of fighter? I'm always trying to find a way to score the points to win or to get the knockout. But the main thing is to walk out the winner at the end! I think everybody prepares for trading differently. In my case, I think because of my competitive nature, I saw the markets as just another event. For me winning is the key: a boxing event, the Harvest Moon Festival, or the Appellate Advocacy Court Championships in law school, which I won after three years of competition.

Q: Jack, this compelling desire to win, where does it come from?

Jack: Who knows? Maybe it's because my mother didn't breast-feed me or something. Maybe it is a fear of failure or rejection. I don't know! You could analyze it in a psychoanalytical way as a Freudian or in a Skinner box way, that I didn't get the food pellet at the right time or I got an electric shock at the wrong time and I was conditioned to want to win! But I always had it. I always wanted to win. I think you can find two people with tremendous comparative instincts in the desire to win, but there's another critical dimension: how you respond to losing and not being successful. Does that response devastate you or does it take you to new heights of trying to figure out what you did wrong and how to prepare in order to be victorious? I think that's essential in trading. I was always committed to finding out new ways to success at trading and everything else!

Q: When you were trading on the floor, how did you prepare yourself?

Jack: I think I just always had the intuitive feeling that winning was a protracted experience in trading and not a one-time thing. Once you can adjust to that and truly understand it's the whole game that counts, then you can look at the market in an objective way.

It isn't a daily thing, because nobody can be a daily winner. You develop rules and discipline and an approach. Of course, you also have to know that to win you must create a set of standards and movements to win and it takes time to do that through trial and error! But the key is to respond as a winner to what happens to you in the market. If the fear of losing is so extraordinary that it inhibits you from moving forward, you cannot be a trader. Also you cannot be an all-or-nothing trader. You can't trade with the attitude that you're going to make a million today or you're going to lose everything you have. That's a disaster! I say you must view trading as a protracted experience and then know how you respond as an individual. I find that people who turn out to be terrible traders are the ones who don't know how to respond to what they would define as a loss. They just don't know how to react. Their fear of losing keeps them in the market too long! It puts them in positions that they wouldn't otherwise have been in. Ultimately you need to have a healthy respect for the market, and the fear of losing cannot be so pervasive in your system that it doesn't allow you to trade to win. You can watch children as they are growing up. You can tell which kid plays not to lose and which one plays all-out to win. There's also the kid who won't dive off the board because he's just too afraid! Or the opposite, the kid who is reckless and gets hurt. To be a successful trader, you need to understand the balance point between being too afraid and too aggressive.

Q: Did you have a defining moment in your own trading career?

Jack: As you know, I got caught in the Hunt fiasco in 1980, and almost went broke. I had what were then huge positions in the market. I learned something very important: I wasn't infallible! Emotionally, it totally stretched me to the limit.

Q: Did you visualize yourself losing or were you just thinking about a new way to win?

Jack: I didn't think of losing. I just thought of how I could get my life adjusted to living in a different way, going back to law or whatever. I realized that this was not the end of the world—it was just the end of trading!

Q: You thought you were out the game.

Jack: Yes, and I really couldn't do much about it. It wasn't like I was using a trading technique that wasn't successful. I was locked in the market! It was out of my control. The market went limit down three days in a row. There were thousands offered. I had limit positions and I was just getting destroyed every day. I was down over $1 million. I was more concerned with just getting through that experience in an emotionally healthy way. I resorted to using psychological techniques to keep myself mentally sound at home and wherever else and not be crazy. I was thinking about adjusting to a new way of life. I was thinking to myself, I'm going to get through it and this isn't the end of the world. All of a sudden the market loosened up, and I made some fabulous trades and what was going to be an astounding loser I turned into a $100,000 winner within 48 hours.

Q: So you go through this emotional upheaval, which you see as a defining moment in your own trading career. You managed to trade out of a huge loss and turn it around into a winner. What did you learn from that experience?

Jack: Never to get in that kind of position again; and that if the worst happened I would still be whole, I would be there to play the game the next day and use my skills. I learned that to trade limit positions was not a wise thing to do. To risk everything on one trade is something I vowed I'd never do anymore.

Q: What about emotionally?

Jack: I had been in difficult situations in my life before that. There have been many other times when I had to reach down deep within myself and try to deal with pain and adversity, so that certainly wasn't the first time. I learned to go back to the well again and rely on those strengths to get myself emotionally whole. It's like what I was saying before about winning: It isn't what outwardly happens to a person; the critical factor is how they respond. That's why some people commit suicide and others reinvent themselves and become more successful than they had ever been before!

Q: What were you telling yourself when it looked like you were going to go broke?

Jack: I kept telling myself that no matter what I would still fig- ure out a way to win. And a winner can be defined in various ways. If I ended up pumping gas, I could still define it as a winner, because I would be happy. You know, at certain points you change your definition of what is a "winner."

There's a book by Abraham Maslow, *The Hierarchy of Needs.* If you're at a point in your life where you're surrounded by luxury items, then securing basic food, clothing, and shelter is not the main issue. But if you lose all of those trappings, you go back to those basic needs. You start to change your definition of winning. Winning at that point, for me, was having a pleasant day, being happy, reading some interesting things, and going through life untroubled. After you satisfy basic needs, then you go to the next level. Winning then may be defined as making a big bang in the market. What I'm saying is I have always been committed to winning at whatever need level I was at at a particular time in my life. Who knows where that comes from? Experiencing a lot of adversity in my childhood, maybe! The important thing for me has always been figuring out a way to come out of this, on my feet, with the victory ribbon.

Q: You've had an incredible life. In many ways, you personify the American dream. You came from very humble origins and you have achieved tremendous success in many different areas. What is winning for you now?

Jack: That's a good question. Today's a very emotional day for me because Bill Brodsky, the president of the Chicago Mercantile Exchange, announced that he is leaving.

I have a tremendous amount of affection for Bill. We worked so closely together, it's like losing a big part of myself even though he'll be working just down the street. So today winning takes on a different dimension. Winning today is just accepting the situation for what it is and trying to progress as an institution. To keep the whole exchange moving forward the way it has for the last 15 years. For me today, that is winning. Yesterday I might have said that winning was doing something great for my firm. Basically, what it comes down to is being successful in all the things that you want. I think that's winning, and I want a lot of different things! I want my kids to do well and be happy.

Q: Do you want your kids to become traders?

Jack: That's a good one.

Q: When I interviewed you for *The Innergame of Trading,* you said that you didn't want your kids to be traders because you felt there was just too much pain involved in trading. Is that still your feeling?

Jack: You know you can't protect your children from everything, but I think trading can be inordinately painful.

Q: Of course, pain can be found in all walks of life.

Jack: Yeah, but the point is that I know the pain here! I'm not so sure about the pain in other walks of life. And the other thing is I really want my children to find their own ways. I don't want them to think that dad wants them to be a trader. I have one child who I think would want to gravitate toward trading, but it could be destructive for him because of his personality right now. He's still young, but I think I can see how his personality is going to develop.

Q: What is it about his personality that you think may not make him suitable for trading?

Jack: I think he could be very emotionally upset because he's so competitive. He doesn't like to lose. I mean, nobody likes to lose, but he really has trouble accepting loss.

Q: Sounds a little bit like his dad!

Jack: Yeah, but he doesn't really know how to take the loss and then move on, to build on it.

Q: Jack, I saw you in the early days in the trading pit. You didn't like to lose either. You were a pretty scrappy guy!

Jack: But he might go in the corner and brood about it and possibly develop a hatred or anger—I never did that. In actuality, I don't know how he will develop, but I do think there are other things he can do with his life where that particular tendency won't get exaggerated. In trading that tendency can get tremendously magnified.

Q: What do you think distinguishes you from all the other players in the market?

Jack: I see myself as a person with a tremendous work ethic. I also have a huge appetite for a broad spectrum of interests and I am able to operate effectively in many different arenas: the business world, the social world, and the cultural world. I love new challenges and adventure. I'm a trader. I own a trading firm and I'm chairman of the Chicago Mercantile Exchange, which I've been heading for 15 years. I'm also very adaptable. Being chairman has changed over the years. It's a completely different paradigm today than it was 15 years ago. I was chairman in 1980, but it is a very different position today.

Q: Is the desire to win as strong as it used to be?

Jack: Absolutely! It's as strong today as it has ever been. I'm out to win, but if I lose I'm able to take a defeat and move on. The board of directors election is in January. If I lose, it'll be painful, but I'm prepared to deal with it just like in 1980. Just like I did during the Hunt fiasco. I'll move on and do something else and enjoy life. I think I could really get myself into a mind-set to enjoy life growing tea roses! I really think I could.

I might enjoy being a Buddhist monk, just getting into that frame of mind . . . getting into the inner self, the real me!

Q: But you'd want to be the winningest Buddhist monk in the Western world, right?

Jack: Yeah, I'd have the biggest prayer wheel that went around the fastest!

CHAPTER 3

Rocket Man

Mike Dever

*Mr. Dever is president and CEO of Brandywine
Asset Management, a commodity trading
adviser managing $200 million.*

Q: What first attracted you to trading?

Mike: Well, I was first drawn to trading in 1979. I was watching the gold market go up and just decided at that point to buy some gold options. I had an interest in markets and math and liked tracking them long before that. When I was kid, I'd spread out the *Wall Street Journal* on the living room floor. I remember going through it and just looking at the new highs and lows and trying to figure out what this was all about. Truthfully, I don't know if it was more the mathematical side or the financial side, but it was just something that was always part of me.

Q: Was it the enjoyment of puzzle solving or game playing?

Mike: Very much so. Although playing the game is only fun if you play to win. Actually, later on, like ten years after I started trading, one of the things we tried to do with my discretionary trading was treat it as if it were a video game. I set up risk management that was totally independent of me at a desk downstairs in my office where someone else handled the actual trade entry. My job was to sit there and say, buy or sell this or that market—not worrying about the quantities necessarily. That was handled systematically by the risk management software, so it really is sort of a puzzle. You know, it is a big game.

Q: Did you enjoy playing games as a kid?

Mike: It's funny you ask, because not that much. I mean I can remember playing certain games, for instance, I really got into Risk. I loved playing that game.

Q: It doesn't sound too much different from what you're doing right now!

Mike: Good point!

Q: What was it about Risk that you liked so much?

Mike: I could dominate the whole world in one shot! I could do it in an afternoon. As you know, it takes a little longer now. So I guess I really did enjoy playing games when I was playing them, but I would never really go out of my way to play games. A lot of my friends would play cards and I never really had any interest in that.

Q: Well, if I may, I'm going to focus on Risk for a second, because I do think it's an interesting point. Was it playing the game of Risk or was it the idea that you could financially dominate the world that you found so attractive?

Mike: It's hard to say, because I know I don't set out and say to myself, "Oh, I'm going to play a game or financially dominate the world." I mean I really don't usually have that much interest in games, but once I start playing a game, it is totally engrossing.

Q: Does trading still have that same attraction for you? I mean now it's—what, 18 years later. Is it still the game playing and the risk taking that excites you?

Mike: In actuality, trying to maintain a level of excitement and be a successful trader has a lot of negatives. One of the things I had to learn a number of years ago was that I had to treat trading less like an exciting game that emotionally encompasses my life and more like something analytical. Which is to say, more like a business than a game. I mean, I still want to have fun. I still want to enjoy what I'm doing and really have my heart in it. So I wake up in the morning with new ideas, and I live it, but I don't want to get as caught up in it as if it were just a game.

Q: Is that the math part of your background calling for recognition?

Mike: Yes, I think so. I think I am pretty analytical. I mean, I love math, I love science. I have always liked the scientific approach to things. I was usually pretty good at looking at something and saying, objectively, whether it was right or wrong. From my standpoint with trading, if I treat it like that, it works out great. If I treat it more like, "Well, I'm doing this and it's kind of fun," it would be a little too easy for me to get caught up in the frenzy and excitement and forget the seriousness of it.

Q: Would it be fair to say that your initial attraction to trading has changed and you are currently less motivated by the excitement and more by the analytical aspects of trading?

Mike: Absolutely, that's true.

Q: What do you think it is about trading that makes it so fascinating?

Mike: I think most people view trading as the ideal livelihood. You know, you can set your own hours, work at your own pace. Of course, there's nothing physically challenging about it. It's just an easy way to make money!

Q: We know otherwise, don't we?

Mike: Yes, it doesn't really work that way! But I think it's more than just hard work. Of all the different things that I've ever done, trading is by far the most challenging, because it's something that you can't force to work. You can't just work twice as many hours or throw extra people at it and make it successful. It requires specific skills. When I was ten years old, I started a little company called STAR. It stood for Scientific Team of Aviation Research. My brother and I would make and sell rocket plans.

Q: Shooting rockets off into outer space and playing Risk. Sounds like the perfect background for a trader!

Mike: It might be. You know, I constantly like new challenges, learning new things. I would get incredibly bored if I went home and watched TV every night. So the main attraction of trading for me is that it's always new. There's nothing that's the same one day to the next. I've talked to people who were always trying to find out what they wanted to do in life. With me, it was a matter of how many lives I could fit into just this one! I've always had so many things I wanted to do. I've been fortunate that I've had a fascination with trading from a young age, and became addicted enough early on to have spent the last 18 years focused on building that interest into a successful business.

Q: Do you think great trading is more of a learned skill or a natural talent?

Mike: I've heard people talk about a particular trader and say how, you know, he was a natural, a born trader. That the person had an intuitive sense of the markets. But frankly, I think intuition without experience is really just good luck. Some people do start trading and immediately make money. Others will say that they were born to trade. From my viewpoint they were lucky. Intuition is not innate. It is simply the instinctual processing of accumulated knowledge. It grows from experience, and that's what really forms the basis of consistently successful trading.

Q: How did you actually start trading? I mean, what was your first trading experience?

Mike: I can give you the good and the bad on that. I started out, as I said earlier, with the gold market. I found out gold options would give me a bigger position with less money, and I thought, "Hey, that's kind of neat." So I bought gold options, and they immediately went sharply lower.

Q: What was the price level of gold then?

Mike: It was in the 300 range. It was right before the big run up to gold's peak.

Q: So this must have been around 1979?

Mike: It was July of 1979.

Q: Yeah, I traded gold on the floor then. Quite a market!

Mike: Yeah, what a wild time! Man! Well, I bought it and it dropped. All I could think of was the loss because it was a lot of money for me at the time, maybe a few hundred dollars, but it seemed like a fortune, and all I wanted to do was get my money back!

Q: Just break even, right?

Mike: Yes! Luckily gold ran up and I got out. It showed me that this can work. Of course, I wasn't sure then how it worked, but I became totally absorbed and began studying, living, and dreaming markets. Soon after, I opened up an account that would allow me to trade futures. I had some money from a car I had just sold. I used that to start trading with. In six months I ran my trading account from $5,000 to over $60,000. Then in one week I lost $80,000. Suddenly I was $20,000 in the hole!

Q: You know, that's not an uncommon experience; I've heard it many times before.

Mike: Yeah, but for me it was quite an initiation. However, what I started to realize from this experience was that it was my basic personality that set me up for this kind of result. The fact that I am super-competitive, thinking I can ram stuff through and make it work. So I guess what I'm saying is that it was a good experience overall, because I learned something about the markets but more importantly about myself. I also realized that trading was what I wanted to do for a living.

Q: At that point, was it the idea that you could do well, or was it the challenge of getting out of difficult situations that kept you in the game?

Mike: I think it was a combination of the two. You know, I had evidence that I could make money trading. Regardless of whether it was skill or luck, I knew it was possible. At the same time, I hated quitting something where I wasn't successful and that more than anything really drove me.

Q: So you felt you could begin trading and be successful at it? Like coming back from a losing play in Risk?

Mike: Yeah, I think that's right. I never wanted to be in a position at the end of my life thinking, "Oh, I wish I had done that." I'd much rather know I tried, even if it meant having to say, "Boy, did I screw that up." Although I had dug myself a hole, I also had the confidence to believe that I could pull myself out of any hole.

Q: So how did you do it? And how did you pay back your $20,000 debit?

Mike: I was getting tons of credit card applications in the mail. They were coming in left and right, and I used every one of them.

Q: I have heard this from a number of traders. I mean this doesn't surprise me in the least. I've heard it countless times before from traders who went through exactly the kind of experience you just described.

Mike: Is that right? I almost hate to say it, because I don't want to encourage other people to do it. At the same time I sold practically everything I owned: my bicycle, stereo, motorcycle, essentially anything I could get a few dollars for. But I mean, that's what really financed my recovery.

Q: You believed so strongly in yourself that you felt you would be able to cover any losses.

Mike: Maybe once or twice in my life I've thought, "Boy, this is really stupid. I really screwed up here." But at the same time I was saying to myself, "I can make it through this." I've never lived very expensively and my personal financial needs were always rather small, so the losses never had that much impact on my overall lifestyle. Losses were much more damaging psychologically than financially.

Q: I think many traders, myself included, have had similar experiences and thoughts. One of the reasons that I've chosen to write this book is to illustrate just this point. Successful trading isn't like getting on an airplane and arriving at the destination of choice: high-performing profitable trading. It usually doesn't work that way. There are always a couple of severe storms on the way, and you know, sometimes you have to, as in my case, go down and, as a friend of mine would say, "analyze the wreckage" before you're ready to fly again.

Mike: But you have to be totally objective in your analysis; otherwise, you'll just keep crashing over and over again.

Q: And did you crash again?

Mike: Yes.

Q: What was it like?

Mike: Each time seemed a little bigger, with bigger stakes.

Q: Bigger ups and bigger downs?

Mike: Yes. But even though I had a couple of larger losses—from which I more quickly recovered—they were less damaging than the initial one.

Q: They were less damaging psychologically?

Mike: Exactly, but also the monetary damage. Not in dollar terms, but at least relative to my ability to recover.

Q: I don't know if you would agree with this, but I have learned much more from my losses than from gains in the market.

Mike: Oh, absolutely, absolutely! You don't reflect on the gains; you reflect on the losses, and the key issue is how you reflect on them! If you sit there and say, "Oh well, the market really screwed me," or something like that, obviously you've gained nothing from the experience. But if you can analyze your behavior—why you did what you did—and try to come up with a way to prevent it from occurring again, you've learned a hell of a lot.

Q: Speaking to that point, what do you think is your greatest strength as a trader?

Mike: Well, I think being objective about my own faults. I think that's a very big strength. As I mentioned before about being in the hole: The challenge is figuring out exactly what it was that caused it. I knew it was me, and a couple times when it first happened and I'd have losses, I thought that I was able to pinpoint the actual cause. People say if you do something once, it's a mistake, that's fine. You do it twice, it's stupid. Well, I did things more than twice, and I don't think it was necessarily stupid, but I think it was learning to really identify the internal fault that would cause it to happen, what part of my personality was responsible. And that took time.

Q: What did you come up with?

Mike: I think my virtues are my vices. I think my perseverance, my drive, my self-confidence, and especially my ability to always look at something and say, "Yep, I can make this work," is exactly the wrong attitude to have as a trader. I mean, you can't make something work if you're fighting what the market is.

Q: So how did you use that insight to improve your own trading?

Mike: By identifying how I had to trade and making that personality characteristic a strength and negating it as a vice. What I did was realize that my approach to trading would have to be much more systematic than I originally had envisioned. I could go out and develop systematic approaches that built on the experiences that I had as a discretionary trader, but day-to-day I couldn't allow myself to make trading decisions. My strength is developing strategies using enormous discretion and intuition in their development and then applying them systematically in the marketplace.

Q: I recently read the article that you wrote on developing trading systems (*MAR Newsletter,* July 1996), and I couldn't be in more agreement with you when you say that for a trading system to really have merit, the internal logic of the system has to make sense rather than to try to curve-fit it to a specific technical or tactical game plan.

Mike: Yes, the software tools are out there that make it real easy to develop systems incorrectly.

Q: I was wondering if you could elaborate on that point.

Mike: Sure. I think there are two ways to develop a system. One is to try to mine data to find a result and then develop a system around it. That's sort of starting backwards, as I view it. The second way is to start with a basic concept that provides a valid basis for providing an inherent return, then develop a system based on that concept. And that's really where the discretionary trading experience comes in. In identifying the valid concepts. You're sitting there and you're analyzing markets and you realize from trading experience how certain things operate in the market, certain interactions. And you can take those experiences and systematize them, quantify them. The point is, you turn these ideas into a system rather than the backwards approach, which is saying, "Well, I'm going to try a bunch of different parameters and different things and throw them at the historical data." I think, just like with any scientific principle, you start with a hypothesis, and then you run it through valid testing to determine whether it's effective, and that's the approach that we take with developing the systems that we trade.

Q: If I can switch to a more personal topic, what effect has trading had on your marriage?

Mike: Well, I've only been married two-and-a-half years. My wife knew me four years before we got married.

Q: Did she need four years to decide whether to marry a trader?

Mike: She had some time to really know what she was getting into. In actuality, it's really been easier for her since we've been married, because when we were dating, in addition to our systematic trading, I was still involved in making day-to-day discretionary trading decisions. I had quote machines at home and in the car and at the office, and it was pretty much an around-the-clock process. I didn't just trade during the day; I traded every market that was available around the world. I mean, she could tell you a lot of stories about all the dinners that we had that were programmed around the Japanese lunch hour. Almost every dinner we had was around 10:00, 10:30 at night, because that's when the markets were quiet in Japan.

Q: You had your dinner when there was a lull in the Azuki bean market!

Mike: Yeah, we do trade that one. Fortunately, now I have the systems and a staff that follows these markets for me. So I guess for the first couple of years we were dating, she had to put up with a lot but made the decision to marry me anyway, so now it's easy.

Q: I'm sure she feels she made the right trade.

Mike: Well, she'd better!

Q: Do you think traders are different from other people?

Mike: Well, I think successful traders are different from other people.

Q: Do you think we process information differently? A friend of mine who's a physician made a comment to this effect the other night. We were going to a restaurant together with our wives—and he and his wife were studying the menu deciding what to get—and I think as traders, and maybe it's just an individual thing, but I think we process information very rapidly because we are in the habit of making split-second decisions. So I quickly looked at the menu. I looked in all the necessary categories—appetizer, entrée, beverage, and dessert—and I knew exactly what I wanted. The waiter came, and the order was placed.

Mike: You know, that's funny. Kim, my wife, always used to say when we ordered in a restaurant, "Have you decided what you want?" And I would say, "No." But the second the waiter would arrive, I'd know exactly what I wanted.

Q: Exactly. You want perfect execution?

Mike: Yeah, when he was there, I made up my mind, I was done. I think there's another important point to be made. A lot of good traders, when looking at a bunch of facts, can debate both sides of an argument equally well. Whereas most people get caught up on only one side. They see it one way, and that's it. I think the best traders can debate it either way, which is to say they argue it with themselves.

Q: But ultimately they have to decide.

Mike: Of course! But they have the ability of looking at both sides before they make a decision. They can make an equally convincing argument to somebody else on either side, I believe. So that when they resolve it for themselves internally they know they are making the right decision. Not necessarily profitable, but nonetheless right!

Q: I think that's a really good point. So in other words, to use the restaurant metaphor, they may know the relative merits of being long or short the bouillabaisse, but they already know in their mind that they're ordering the cabbage soup.

Mike: That's right. They're long cabbage. But they can tell *you* why you shouldn't be eating it.

Q: I often say that to traders—that I can't remember having a trade-on—I mean, something that ultimately turned out to really be a good trade, where there were not a half a dozen people who gave me cogent reasons why this was the worst thing I could possibly be doing. Ultimately, you need that kind of independence of mind to be able to say, I understand your argument and why you find it so compelling, but this is what I have to do in this situation. Make the trade and live with the consequences.

Mike: We were doing that this year (1996) when the big grain market was coming to an end in April. A bunch of our systems kicked in that were either sentiment- or volatility-based and we started liquidating long positions.

Q: Yes.

Mike: And some of the markets were limit up at the time. The systems were indicating to sell. Our traders are calling the floor and they're saying, "Oh, you know, they're up limit. They could be limit up again for the next couple of days." And of course, we were selling. Before we completed our trades, the markets had all come off limit and were heading lower. That was the end of the bull move. I think it's just so neat when you can see a system operating that way, going against the tide, but based on sound, tested logic. It's so rare for most people to do that!

Q: I can remember as a novice trader being in the pit and seeing a wire house broker trying to fill a very large order. It was a price order, and there were about ten locals standing around at the time, asking each other, "Why would anybody want to sell the market at this level?" The biggest local in the pit at the time walked over to the broker and simply said "sold." The market immediately went down, and traded limit down, I think for the next two days. I learned a very important lesson that day. All you have to say is "buy or sell." You don't have to wonder or question why somebody else is trying to do something.

Mike: That's right. Not everybody is making the right decision.

Q: But to return to your point, you must possess that independence of mind to know that it's okay to go your own way and know what your own way is.

Mike: I think you learn to identify the people that you should fade and the people that you should copy. Some people are also a really good emotional gauge. I have a friend, and I can almost count on that when he's excited about a market, that it's just naturally ready to peak. You know, a market, an idea, or just a trend. He's just really good at calling market tops that way. He's my human indicator.

Q: My old office was outside what they used to call in the old days a "board room," a big trading room filled with brokers and retail clients. When a market would really heat up, phones would be ringing like there was no tomorrow. You could just feel the intensity. I always felt that we were close to a top of the market. Many years later, I heard a trader on the floor say something that kind of reiterated that same sentiment during high-volume times in a market. He said, "When the ducks are quacking, you've got to feed them." If you kind of look at the quacking as distribution, it makes perfect sense. When the ducks need to be fed you must give them supply. Also, from a purely auditory standpoint, when you're next to a board room, and those phones are ringing, and the public just can't wait to jump in, it's usually a pretty good indicator to reevaluate your own position!

Mike: Yeah, that's right. It gets back to the idea of distinguishing the noise from the signal.

Q: What was your worst moment ever in the market? Hopefully there was just one.

Mike: It's hard to say because at the time when there are problems, it seems like that is the worst, but I'd say for me the worst I ever had and what led to our reevaluating our trading and becoming systematic traders was our experience in 1987. The reason is that I was extremely bearish on the U.S. stock market at the time and going into October I got a little bit sideways on my short position and, in fact, I was actually long right before the crash. So here I was in a position that I didn't want to be in during the crash of 1987. That was probably about the worst experience. I had written articles on why the market was ready to crash, I saw something happening and not only did I miss it, but I ended up on the wrong side of the market!

Q: How did you work your way out of that?

Mike: I made the decision that I was in this game for the long haul and what I had to do was reevaluate everything I was doing so that I would not be in that situation again.

Q: So basically the way you got through the crash was to use it as a learning experience to completely turn around your trading approach?

Mike: Exactly. My decision at that point was that I was going to build on my own strengths as a trader and create a systematic approach. I hired a guy by the name of Fred Gehm, who wrote a book called *Commodity Market Money Management.* I was looking to him to assist us in developing money management guidelines, and we put together a staff of people and started using a lot of interns to develop a systematic model based on my discretionary trading experience and market knowledge.

We were in retrospect pretty fortunate. I had enough cash flow going and it was one of those things where I started saying to myself again, okay, when I look back in 20 years, what will I wish I had done?

I was 30 years old at the time and wanted to be able to look back later on with no regrets that I did the right thing. So I committed to making the investment in the research. I knew the process and I think the strength I always had in my personality was that I had an intuitive sense about what had to be done to get myself back on my feet. I mean, I stood there and said, this is exactly what I have to do to do it right. And I knew even when I wasn't doing something right, when I was heading in the wrong direction. So I kind of kept thinking, well, I will just keep doing it till I get it right. I really made the commitment at that point to utilize the best of two distinct approaches. I guess you'd call it the intuitive or discretionary component, which we merged quantitatively with the risk management side. The challenge of course was to balance our strategy given all the markets we traded.

Q: What was your best moment in the market? I feel we've spent too much time on the worst moments.

Mike: I don't think it has arrived yet. You know, I've certainly had plenty of very good moments. But I think the really informative experiences are when things don't go according to plan. I've learned so much from the bad moments so in a way I have a hard time thinking of best moments. It's not that they're not fulfilling.

Q: Do you think it's your natural resistance to a feeling of complacency?

Mike: Maybe that's it! When I'm doing well, I'm always looking over my shoulder, trying to stay ahead. I'm always thinking "What can we do to prevent problems in order to keep things going?"

Q: Of course that's one of the essential strengths that you need to possess. The ability to be able to look over your shoulder.

Mike: My wife has mentioned a couple of times that in her opinion my personality's pretty stable. I'm not somebody who gets really excited about things. It takes a lot to get me really excited, and it's not that I'm not enjoying things! I guess even when I am excited, I don't display it outwardly like a lot of people do. That's why it's very difficult for me to say what was my best moment.

I think I just know that there are these troughs and then you come out of them. Probably the best I feel is when I come out of these periods. Everything after that is sort of muted. You know you have suffered and then you come back from it.

Q: I think that's really an important point. When I interviewed Jack Sandner, he made that point in a very compelling way. He said, for him, being a good trader was being able to deal with life's adversity. At first I thought that response was pretty general, but if you know anything about Jack's background, he's really faced his share!

It's just knowing that you can come out of the hole and as the lyric goes "Pick yourself up, dust yourself off and start all over again."

Q: What was your funniest experience in the market?

Mike: I had a client for a brief time—I should have known better before taking him on—but I did anyway. We had a number of conversations and once with a very straight face, he told me how people were always out to get him personally when he was trading. And of course this is stuff every trader feels, but we know in reality the market is basically impersonal. But this guy really believed the whole thing was very, very personal.

You know, wherever his stops were, the market was there to pick him off, intentionally. Like, who the hell cares about him, right? But what really got to me was when he said, "And you know, they have different quote machines from you and me. These machines that tell them exactly where the market's going to be!"

Q: Sometimes it feels that way, doesn't it?

Mike: Oh, yes, of course, you know, everything he's saying, I'm thinking, "Yeah!" You know, I mean obviously I've had that thought but any normal person quickly reminds himself that this kind of thinking is totally irrational. This guy just could not differentiate between how the markets make us feel and what is obviously not real.

Q: We have all had those feelings, but for him, he was living in his own personal version of trading hell!

Mike: It was weird.

Q: I remember many years ago, when I was trading on the exchange floor, on a lark I bought a five-lot of bellies and as soon as I bought it, the market immediately ran up to the limit. There was a new runner there who had seen me make this trade. It was his first or second day, and he couldn't believe that I did that. He gave me this puzzled look. A day or two later, I repeated the same sort of trade again in front of the same runner. I mean, we all live for trades like that, right? Unfortunately, they don't happen as often as they should! But anyway the kid walked up to me and asked

"How'd you do that? I've seen you do this two days in a row," and I said, somewhat impishly "Do you see the board? I know the guy behind it who works the lights, and when he is ready to start sending the market up, he winks at me, and I start buying!" You know that explanation seemed to satisfy him. I mean, he'd only been working at the exchange for three or four days, and I remember overhearing him as I walked onto the floor the next day. He pointed me out to another runner and said, "He knows the guy behind the boards who works the lights."

Mike: That's great. That's a good title for your next book.

Q: What has trading taught you about yourself?

Mike: It has taught me that I can usually make anything work if I view it objectively, if I approach it properly. Trading is one of the most challenging things in the world. Some of the other things in life are easy compared to trading in that you have much more control over them. With trading, although from a systems approach you have certain control, there's still an aspect of it that is left to some sort of a chaotic force or random chance, which you can't control. And of course it's really very different from most other businesses or other adventures people take on, you know like learning to fly, racing cars, skiing, things like that. With all that other stuff, you know, the harder you work at it, you're going to get better at it, but that doesn't necessarily apply to trading.

Trading is something that will always be part of me. I think one thing that surprised a lot of people is that when I stopped the discretionary trading, I didn't feel the need to go back to it. I mean discretionary trading really has a unique nature. You really do start to feel like you have a vision of the future or something. There were times when I'd wake up in the morning, and I knew exactly what to do in the market, and everything was just perfect through the day. It just worked! I've had months where it just seemed like day after day after day everything went according to plan. And when you're trading on a discretionary basis, that is great. It's really neat, and I wasn't sure I'd be able to go to a fully systematic method and get that same psychological satisfaction, but I do.

Q: What do you think distinguishes you from other traders?

Mike: I'd like to think that I have a lot of the same traits that the other successful traders have, as far as the ability to view things objectively, view all sides of an argument and quickly come to the right answer. The ability to build on an existing base of knowledge. I don't know that I possess a lot of distinctive qualities.

Q: I'd say that the fact that you haven't identified yourself as being distinct is pretty distinct.

Mike: Is that because everybody's trying to differentiate themselves?

Q: As you know, many successful traders have egos that rival the Taj Mahal, but that goes with the territory.

Mike: I think I'm very confident.

Q: You're so low-key. I sincerely hope the readers get a sense of how laid-back, dare I say humble, your answers are. It seems to me you really do seem to have a very analytical temperament.

Mike: I'm sure I have a big ego, but I'm comfortable with it. I also realize that I'm just a gnat in relation to the whole universe.

Q: Does that take us back to your interest in astronomy, one gnat in relationship to the entire universe?

Mike: As I said earlier, I love astronomy. I love going out in the middle of the night, the world around me is asleep, standing there under a canopy of stars. You feel so insignificant. But I love that feeling. It is a great feeling.

Q: Yes, you feel insignificant, but it's very comforting to know that you are part of a miraculous universe that is all around you.

Mike: It is a very warm feeling knowing you are part of, however small, such an astonishing place.

Q: It sounds to me like that's the way you approach the market, almost as a student of astronomy taking a look through his telescope being awed and analytical by the wonder of it all.

Mike: That's right. I am completely awed by it all. Both the markets and the universe are tremendously fascinating, but at the same time each has their own way of making you feel insignificant. Of course I do realize that to myself I'm highly significant, but not to everybody and not to the universe at large. There is a quote that I really like that came out in the 1980 World Series. It was said by Tug McGraw, the relief pitcher. Somebody asked him how he remained so cool under pressure. And McGraw said, "I

just use the ice ball theory. The ice ball theory is that in five bil-
lion years, the sun will have burned out and the Earth will be one
big ice ball, and who's going to give a damn about my pitching
then?" When you get down to it you might as well go out, do what
it is you want to do, and make damn sure it is the best you possibly can do. Don't get overblown by the significance of it, because
in universal terms it is trivial. And in the end, that will be success.

CHAPTER 4

Solomon's Mind

Solomon Cohen

Mr. Cohen runs CK Partners, Inc., in New York City,
investment advisers to the Gazelle Global Fund Limited.
The Gazelle Fund was the top-performing equities fund in 1995.
Born in London, he studied mathematics at Cambridge
and music at the Guildhall School of Music. He worked at
James Capel & Co. in derivative sales and proprietary
trading before leaving to start his own firm.

Q: What first attracted you to trading?

Solomon: I started trading at the age of 16. But I think to really answer that question, you have to understand the character of the city of London—by which I mean the square mile—where the Stock Exchange, the Bank of England, Lloyds, and most of the other financial institutions are located, in a labyrinth of medieval lanes with names like Bread Street and Pudding Lane, a place with its own police force and governing body.

The city brings together a very odd mix of people: East End boys—I don't mean that in any derogatory sense, just in a descriptive way—people who have come straight from the fruit and vegetable market to deal in stocks and bonds; and very educated upper-class people who have come from schools like Eton; and a third group, Jews. The city is one of the few places where in the past few hundred years Jews came and were able to set up positions to become a very successful and respected group with quite a strong identity. And you had institutions in the city where there were some very clear divisions—a bank like Rothschilds, which was a very Jewish institution, and a bank like Barings, which was very English and blue-blooded; a firm like Smith Brothers and a firm like Cazenove. These different people had to learn how to respect each other and do business together. And the city was a place full of mystery and intrigue and tradition and tribalism; full of danger for the unwary but also offering great rewards for the astute and the daring. And all of this totally fascinated me, and I very much wanted to be a part of this world.

Q: What was the part that you found most fascinating? Was it the dealing aspect of it? Was it making money? Was it the social relationships? Or was it just being part of this great "theater"?

Solomon: Well, part of it was discovering at a young age the idea that things could be traded, transactions could be carried out verbally in things that were totally abstract, and that these dealings could yield forth so much money, money on a scale which is nothing like everyday life. That's something that fascinated me. My interest in mathematics is something which developed after that.

Q: Are you still attracted to trading for the same reasons?

Solomon: The city of London has changed a lot in the last ten years, but it still retains an element of the type of place that it was, but you know, there isn't a trading floor anymore where people congregate to transact business. I would say now that the ability to trade land, buildings, factories, whole workforces anywhere in the world with a phone call or with a touch of a computer button is the ultimate in mathematical abstraction—and to have this at your fingertips on an electronic screen!

Q: What is it about that that you find so fascinating?

Solomon: Well, obviously, there's something immensely powerful about it. I mean, if you had to build a factory, it would take years or a long time to create a company, and now, instantaneously and in an abstract way, you can own it and there's almost no physical side to all of this. It's almost like a virtual world in that everything you do exists really on computer or on paper. It's almost like moving mountains!

Q: Abstract mountains.

Solomon: Yes. Move incredible things really with the strength of a phone call.

Q: Do you think there was anything in your personal background that prepared you for trading? You know, you touched on the math—we haven't yet spoken about the music—and you have mentioned your fascination with the dealing part of it. So what specifically would you say is unique about your experience that prepared you to trade?

Solomon: I seem to have been born with some sort of instinct.

Q: An intuition?

Solomon: Yes. I remember visiting the Eiffel Tower with my parents when I was seven years old. When I came down, realizing that the ticket my parents purchased hadn't been collected, I went up to somebody, and offered them the ticket. In actuality, I just meant to give it to them, but they gave me money for it!

Q: Well, that wasn't so much a question of converting the abstract. It was more converting the concrete into cash!

Solomon: I can't really tell you where that came from. Perhaps my ancestors were the money changers in the temple in Jerusalem if you go back a few thousand years. You know, that's where the name "Cohen" comes from, I mean, officiating in the temple; I don't know about money changing!

Q: Of course, the Hebrew translation for Cohen is priest. The Cohens were the people who officiated at the holy temple. Are you saying that this part of your background prepared you for trading? I mean, do you feel like there's something religious or culturally influenced about what you do?

Solomon: Well, the money changing was a joke.

Q: Right, but in my experience a lot of truth gets expressed in joke form.

Solomon: Yes. *Priest* is actually not the most accurate translation of Cohen. They actually would have served about two days out of the year, but the rest of the time they were more in the role of sage, judge, or doctor. Their obligation was pretty much to serve the community.

Q: Yes, I know my ancestors served your ancestors! My ancestors were Levites, so way back when, we ministered to your needs!

Solomon: They're the ones that used to sing as well.

Q: That's right. There's a whole biblical book written about us—Leviticus.

Solomon: Well, you're also quite right. I think the fact that Jews were very respected in the city, hired for their skills, their financial skills, is something that stood out for me.

Q: So you saw this in a personal sense as an opportunity perhaps for individual recognition or achievement?

Solomon: Yes, I would say that is definitely true.

Q: I must say, Solomon, I've heard that same sentiment expressed on a number of occasions. There is a trader whom I interviewed for *The Innergame of Trading,* Jeffrey Silverman; you may know of him—who basically said something very similar to what you've expressed. He grew up in Omaha, Nebraska, in the 1950s, and said being Jewish in Nebraska then did not present too many opportunities. What really opened his eyes for the first time was when he was in grade school, and he read the biography of Bernard Baruch. He said his life changed from that day forward. So I have heard similar reports before. I guess all I was trying to establish was that this connection was significant for you and who you are today.

Solomon: Yes, I think at that age and at that time, that's definitely true.

Q: Is it still true?

Solomon: Not really. London has opened up so much, and these divisions really changed quite a lot. In fact, an important aspect of my trading now is the global perspective. So the divisions I spoke about earlier are starting to become blurred and to a large extent don't really exist anymore. They used to be very clear-cut, and that was something that was very striking. As I said before, there were firms that employed no Jews and there were firms that employed mainly Jews.

Q: So is it fair to say in the same sense that Jeff Silverman did that you viewed trading as an avenue that would allow you to cross borders and to go beyond the stereotypical divisions and the arbitrary categories and conventions of the time? I mean, as you were thinking about trading, was that one of the things that it held out for you, the ability to transcend your normal possibilities?

Solomon: I think that came later. It wasn't there initially, because the whole idea of financial markets was still viewed with a certain amount of disdain, I would say. I mean, in England, for a long time, money has been seen as something which is at worst dirty, but definitely not polite.

Q: Well, in my experience, its cleanliness is determined by who possesses it!

Solomon: Well, you know, there was an attitude that money was to be inherited rather than made.

Q: Well of course! One of the worst things you could do from that perspective was actually to earn your own money! It's so much more refined to actually get it from someone else.

Don't get me wrong. I wouldn't have minded inheritance, it just didn't happen for me that way!

Solomon: It is amusing. I mean, the thing that I notice as I travel around the world, and go onto the floor of different markets around the world, is how each society has its own code and set of values and its own way of thinking and doing business. Sometimes it's a strength and sometimes it's a weakness. But now we have traders from one country operating in another, and that's really started to change the entire structure and outlook of indigenous markets.

Q: Let's talk about the Gazelle Global Fund for a second. In 1995 it was up 297 percent and had the distinction of being the top-performing hedge fund in the world. Could you tell me a little bit about the history and thinking behind the fund?

Solomon: Well, in the mid-80s, I worked for James Capel, a large securities firm in London, working with big institutions and helping them to use derivatives in their trading. As I walked around the trading floor I suddenly discovered all these amazing opportunities to make money because I understood what people in different areas of the firm were doing. And so I was able to persuade my boss that I should move to proprietary trading, where I could carry out transactions on behalf of the firm for profit. And after awhile in developing my own strategies and implementing them successfully, I decided to leave and set up my own company. I just thought setting up a hedge fund was the next logical step. In fact, I would say that much of the hedge fund industry, certainly the people coming into that business over the last year or two, are skilled people who have been carrying out proprietary trades for big investment houses, and now that the technology and capital is more easily available, have been able to set up their own firms.

Q: How did you choose the name *Gazelle*?

Solomon: I thought long and hard about a name for the firm. I mean, a name is important.

Q: It doesn't sound very Jewish!

Solomon: Well, you know, there is something in Jewish tradition that the choice of name is supposed to influence outcomes.

Q: I know, but Gazelle sounds too much like a sacrificial offering! I don't know how that relates specifically to a fund.

Solomon: Well, gazelles are elegant...

Q: Fast-moving . . .

Solomon: . . . nimble animals that can leap forward and upward quickly.

Q: Which you've certainly been doing.

Solomon: Yeah, I'm happy to say that that's true.

Q: You mentioned something about your background earlier, the incident where you sold the unused Eiffel Tower ticket; I think it kind of begs a question. Do you think your great trading is more of a natural endowment or a set of learned skills?

Solomon: Ultimately, I think it's both, in the same way that you have to have talent to be a musician, but you also need training from the hands of the master.

Q: Talk a little bit about your music. You have a master's degree in mathematics from Cambridge, and you also you won a scholarship to the Guildhall School of Music. I've heard you take time out during the trading day to play Beethoven sonatas on your Bechstein piano. Is there any truth to that?

Solomon: Yes, that's absolutely true, and it's so helpful to break up the routine and stress of the day.

Q: It changes your state of mind and allows you to just get focused back on the trading?

Solomon: Yes, absolutely, there's something very spiritual and head-clearing about it.

Q: Let's return to the question of whether you feel trading is more of a learned skill or a natural endowment. You said that you felt in your case it was a combination of the two, so the skill set is as important as the intuition. Is that it?

Solomon: Yes, I think for me that's true. I mean, there are traders that I know who are completely intuitive, and others who are much more scientific.

Q: And they are equally successful?

Solomon: I think the intuitive traders are probably more volatile, their performance is more volatile. The scientific people tend to be more narrowly focused. Then all of a sudden, they'll be taken completely by surprise by something that doesn't conform to their model. I can give you an example of this.

I believe it was 1988, people were coming into the options market in London and paying very extravagant premiums for call options on a large mining company. There was one trader who is extremely well respected in the market, who is regarded as a very clever man, a real expert in a mathematical sense on options. This market maker sold a great deal of these options. According to his model, he sold them at inflated prices. On the other hand, there was another well-known character in the London market—an intuitive trader, it's better not to mention names—who the day before sold these same options. All this happened the day before Yom Kippur, and he decided—he was Jewish—that something didn't look right and he covered the entire position. He hedged his short calls one for one with stock.

On Yom Kippur, a takeover bid came out for that company. And the scientific trader, staying true to his model, lost quite a bit of money. He just lacked the flexibility or intuition to move.

Q: Solomon, over your trading career, are there any memorable characters that stand out?

Solomon: David Heron, my old boss at James Capel, was someone who I respected and admired a great deal.

Q: What is it about him that stood out?

Solomon: I had never seen someone quite like him before. He was immensely successful, and I had the opportunity to observe him at close hand for some time. I was struck by the fact that whatever he was doing, there was always this calm professionalism

about the way that he went about his business—always calm,
everything without emotion. Never trading and then keeping his
fingers crossed hoping things would work out, but rather having
considered all the possibilities, so that when something went
wrong, it was an outcome that had already been considered.
There was something rather panther-like about the way in which
he operated, very sleek and sure-footed.

Q: Panther-like rather than gazelle-like?

Solomon: Yes, I would say that that's true.

Q: In what respect? I think of both gazelles and panthers as
being sure-footed, sleek, and elegant and moving quickly and
upwardly, but there certainly is something more predatory about
a panther. Is that what you were trying to imply?

Solomon: I think there's an element of that. I'm not sure I want
to say too much more on that subject. That's the aspect of markets
I find least attractive!

Q: The predatory aspects.

Solomon: Yes.

Q: When you were at James Capel, you witnessed the 1987
stock market crash.

Solomon: Actually, I had left a month before.

Q: What was your response to the crash?

Solomon: I wasn't completely taken by surprise. We had had a
very sharp fall in the London market at the end of July—I think it
was associated with bad trade figures. The market then re-
bounded, and I decided to sell out. If you were paying close attention, there were a lot of indications that the astronomical rise in
the market was not going to last forever. Having said that, I must
add that when the crash actually came, it was quite a shocking experience. To witness this meltdown environment was very scary!
It was just the idea that the unthinkable can actually happen.

Q: And that there was opportunity in that situation?

Solomon: Well, yes, of course. There was opportunity in that
situation, but I think ever since I've been mindful that there's always a possibility of something of that kind occurring, and therefore when I stretch my dealings, rather than making a great deal
of money nine times out of ten and then going bankrupt on the

tenth time, it's better to make a little bit less each time but to take your place at the table.

Q: As they say on the trading floors of Chicago, just make sure you have enough to be able to walk through that turnstile tomorrow. That's the idea, isn't it?

Solomon: Yes, because once you're out, you're out for good.

Q: What do you think is your greatest strength as a trader?

Solomon: It's the combination of all the skills that I have. There's an intuitive feel for the market and the ability to think very mathematically and precisely, understanding the psychology of markets and of the individuals who are behind the markets. Recognizing that information is not evenly distributed across the markets, and knowing with analyzed information I can usually come up with the right conclusion.

Q: What do you think is your greatest weakness as a trader?

Solomon: That is a very powerful question. My greatest weakness is possessing unrelenting high standards.

Q: That's a good weakness to have!

Solomon: In some ways.

Q: What untoward consequences do you identify?

Solomon: Well, I think it means overachieving in some areas at times to the expense of overall happiness.

Q: Well, you know, your investors are happy that you have this kind of weakness, because if you didn't, maybe they would only be looking at 97 percent or 197 percent return instead of the 297 percent return you delivered. So I don't think they're complaining about your high standards, do you?

Solomon: Probably not. But the people who work for me or do business with me are!

Q: Let's talk a little about that, Solomon. What effect does your trading have on your social relationships? We haven't discussed if you're married or not.

Solomon: Only to Gazelle.

Q: What's that?

Solomon: Only to the Gazelle.

Q: Oh, to the Gazelle! It's sounding more and more Jewish as you mention its name!

Solomon: Let's hope no one accuses me of bestiality. I should make it clear we're talking about a virtual gazelle!

The way I tend to work is like a musician who will prepare intensely for a concert, give a performance, and then take time off. I tend to have intense bursts of concentration where I give everything. I can only sustain that for a certain period of time, and that's why I run an event-driven fund as opposed to something which requires a lower level of attention or dedication consistently day-in, day-out. The consequence of that is, there are many times when I have to be up at 2:00 or 3:00 in the morning. There have been periods where I actually traded London, New York, and Australia during the same day. That is a little bit tough trading three time zones. But then at the end of that trade, once I've brought the deal to a successful conclusion and we've earned a good rate of return, I can then give myself the luxury of a break where I will have quite a bit of time to do whatever I want.

I think that the biggest complaint of a lot of successful people is that no matter how much money they make or how good they are, they're still going to be limited to perhaps four weeks of vacation a year and still have to put in incredibly long days. And the only time people ever really get to do something wonderful—go to South America or go on a safari or something—is when they change jobs or get a few months off in between.

Q: What is the most wonderful thing you've ever done?

Solomon: I think the most wonderful thing I've ever done was spend six months traveling around the world, and as I went around to all the different places, New York, Chicago, San Francisco, Los Angeles, Hong Kong, Tokyo, Sydney, and so on, I always followed the same formula: I met people that I knew in the markets and I went onto the trading floors of the markets in those places. I also looked up distant relatives—amazingly I've got them in a multitude of places—as well as meeting people and seeing friends. That experience changed me. Just as a result of that experience I left London and decided to live in New York.

Q: How did you change?

Solomon: Well, if you spend most of your life in the place where you were born, that's pretty much all you know. As you travel, you start to put your own culture in some kind of perspective.

Q: You had mentioned earlier that trading gave you the ability to cross intellectual borders and categories, and now you are saying as a result of your travels, of crossing physical borders, you developed a deeper sense of who you are and how to operate. Is that correct?

Solomon: It was crossing borders that gave me new opportunities to trade. That trip really transformed the way I thought of doing business, by making me aware of opportunities in markets all over the world—seeing similarities and noticing differences; efficiencies and inefficiencies; strengths and weaknesses on a psychological level, on a business level. This global perspective, it's just been immensely valuable for me and has given me a sense of what I can accomplish.

Q: What has been the funniest moment for you as a trader?

Solomon: I think one of the funniest things that occurred to me was at James Capel. There was a bank of 30 dealers who would transact whatever you wanted to do with other participants in the market. I approached the desk with an order, and before I'd even opened my mouth, the head trader said, "And I'll have a fiver PA," which means, "Whatever Cohen's doing I want to buy 5,000 for my own account not even knowing what the stock is." That really made me laugh!

Q: It must have also made you feel pretty damn proud!

Solomon: The immediate question that popped into my mind was, what if I was about to sell short?

Q: Well, I have a feeling he was going to go short then, don't you?

Solomon: A lot of them didn't really understand what I was doing. They admired me, but I think some people were also afraid of me.

Q: What were they afraid of?

Solomon: I think people are afraid of things that they don't understand or maybe they felt somehow they would be taken advantage of in some way.

There was this dealer—I had spotted a great opportunity in his area which was outside of the product that I traded, and I was trying to explain it to him. And, you know, he kept questioning me and then became quite angry. I just left him. About three weeks later, he came up to me, and he said, "Solomon, do you remember that trade you wanted me to do? Now I understand it! That would have been a marvelous trade." It was something which was mathematical and guaranteed to work out. You see, he was afraid or resistant to consider the logic, reasoning. and structure behind what I was trying to do.

Q: Do you think traders process information differently from most people?

Solomon: Yes, I think we think very quickly and very effectively. We're used to making decisions on the spot because we have to. We have to absorb and process information very rapidly. If we can't get a precise answer to something, we immediately establish a range of possibilities. And I get frustrated if a friend's coming over and I ask, "What time are you coming?" and they say, "I don't know" because I'm used to crisp, efficient answers.

Q: Personally, I hate that also. I mean, I was raised in a family where you could answer "yes" or "no," but you could never answer "I don't know." That was just an unacceptable answer, and it is frustrating when you get it sometimes! A trader needs precision in his responses.

Q: What has trading taught you about yourself?

Solomon: Trading has taught me different things about myself at different times, according to how the situation has gone. It has taught me that I can be very disciplined, that I don't have to have external constraints imposed on me. It's taught me that I'm very self-reliant. Often I can put together the jigsaw puzzle, even though some pieces are missing and will have an insight into a trade which other traders don't perceive. Sometimes I realize I've been arrogant in the way I've done something.

It's interesting how trading teaches us something about ourselves that we don't necessarily want to know but the information is always very instructive.

I am always thinking about my trading. I look back and analyze how things have gone, why I took certain decisions, what I did with information that was available to me, how I have interacted with other people in the marketplace, and it's always a learning experience.

Q: What do you think distinguishes you from everyone else in the market?

Solomon: I am the way that I am. It's something which is completely natural and instinctive. It's not something that I really think about. When I get into a discussion with a broker or a dealer about the way they want to handle a deal, I can see some clear differences between us.

If I had to generalize it, I would say that I think diagrammatically, in terms of abstract structure. Others tend to be more focused on detail, on smaller perspectives. Sometimes I feel like I'm looking at the whole room, while others are squinting through a keyhole.

Q: That's a very interesting way to put it. And the music and the mathematics? Do these give you a greater ability to see the entire room and not get lost squinting in the keyhole?

Solomon: Absolutely, because both mathematics and music are about structure and about the ability to see structures. If you think about algebra and how, you know, we arrive at general solutions to problems, it can be widely applied to a whole range of things. So we're looking for patterns and symmetry, and from there you can work down and apply concepts to individual situations.

Q: And the music?

Solomon: The music is also about structure.

Q: It's about structure, like mathematics, but in this case of music. It's about transcending structure, isn't it?

Solomon: In what way?

Q: Well, I mean music obviously has a structural base, as does mathematics. But to really understand a musical composition in some sense is to go beyond the structure of the piece to its transcendent essence.

Solomon: Well, often people don't see the structure in music. I mean just recently my father was saying, listening to something that Beethoven composed, "God, this is so wonderful. I don't know how somebody could have created this!" In fact, the music represents a combination of creative force, you know, something raw and original; however, there's a pattern which is followed.

And there is a structure and a method to develop the idea musically.

Without this structure, the music would appear without form. It would not be a sonata or a symphony; it would merely be chaotic!

Q: But of course it is this very structure, the key if you will, which allows you to experience the whole room that transcends the structure itself.

Solomon: Yes. An important aspect of music that we haven't touched on is its ability to stir up powerful emotions, which is really the opposite of good trading. You don't want to let your emotions have an impact on your decisions.

Q: So does the actual playing of Beethoven sonatas during the trading day allow you to gratify those emotional needs, so you can approach your trading paradoxically with greater detachment and discipline?

Solomon: Definitely. I think I would go crazy if my entire life was spent in front of a trading screen!

Q: It's nice to sit down in front of a Bechstein also, isn't it?

Solomon: Yeah. It has always been a dream of mine to have one.

Q: Mine, too.

Solomon: Beautiful instruments. But, you know they're not so easy to come by in America.

Q: Neither is a return of 297 percent.

CHAPTER 5

Fly on a Rhino's Back

Timothy McAuliffe

Mr. McAuliffe is a member of the International Monetary Market. He has been a member and floor trader at the Chicago Mercantile Exchange since 1982.

Q: What first attracted you to trading?

Tim: I used to gamble with other traders at racquetball. They were members of the Chicago Board of Trade, Mercantile Exchange, and Board Options Exchange.

Q: So your initial experience with traders was on the racquetball court?

Tim: I belonged to a health club when I first started to play racquetball. It was just for the fun of the game, and then one day an old-time trader, Sammy Carl, took me aside and said, "Timmy boy, you're too old to lace up your sneakers and play for nothing." So I started playing for $5 a game, and it was always double or nothing. Eventually the stakes got up to $7,000 a game with large side bets!

Q: This was against traders?

Tim: Traders and brokers, and given the size of the bets, I was playing with some very successful market makers. At some point, one of the traders suggested that I should try the markets.

Q: How did you go from being a racquetball player to becoming a trader?

Tim: I actually left Chicago and signed a contract to become a professional racquetball player first. I left for two years.

Q: Because you thought there was big money in it?

Tim: Yes, and I enjoyed playing the game. This was 1977; I signed a contract with a club in Miami and moved down there.

Q: How does all this relate to trading?

Tim: In the off-season my brother, Kevin, called me in need of a trading stake.

Q: What was he doing?

Tim: He was going to become a local on the New York Futures Exchange. Kevin wanted me to come up there and work with him. I had two months between tournaments. It was right after the national championships. I decided to go to New York and in about a six-week period, I lost all the money that I had earned in a year from racquetball.

Q: Do you remember your first impression of the market?

Tim: I thought if I could only be one-tenth the trader that I am a racquetball player, I'd be a multimillionaire in no time.

Q: So what would you say was your initial attraction to the market? Was it the competitive aspect of trading?

Tim: Absolutely! That's one of the reasons I stayed in racquetball as long as I did. I came from a huge sports background and had been competitive all my life. I've always enjoyed the adrenaline rush when a game is on the line. Throughout my athletic career, the coach or my teammates always wanted me to take the last shot because when the game is on the line I'm incredibly focused.

Q: I've played basketball with you, and I know you like to take that last shot.

Tim: I'm not afraid to fail. I definitely can miss a last shot, but it's not because I choked or was indecisive. I want the ball in my hand. I don't want it resting in somebody else's. But you have to have discipline too. I think if there is one common trait among all successful traders it is discipline. So although I might want to take the last shot, I'm not going to throw up a brick. And if I've gone zero-for-ten that day, I'm going to call a time out to make sure the best possible shot gets taken. I never forget the object of the game is to take home the victory!

Q: Tim, if there's three seconds to go, and the game depends on you and the ball's in your hand . . .

Tim: I'm not going to ditch the ball. I'm definitely never going to do that! I'm the guy you can rely on to give you the win!

Q: What do you think the public finds so fascinating about trading?

Tim: Actually, the general public doesn't know that much about what's going on down here.

Q: Would you like to offer an insider's view?

Tim: The general public needs to know what trading is all about. For many, it's seen as gambling. The public seems to be enthralled with games of chance that are rampant in this country: lotteries, casinos, riverboats, all that stuff! Trading successfully is not about gambling at all.

From my perspective, if I bet on the Chicago Bears and I'm given 14 points and they're down 21 to nothing at half time, the hundred dollars that I bet is gone. But in trading if I'm real bullish, and the market's just jamming on the downside, I can always turn it around. There's definitely skill involved. It's not just a passive stake. You are an active participant. When I'm talking to young traders, I tell them to make sure to have enough trading capital for tomorrow. Don't put the whole thing on the line. Because if you do, you won't be able to play the game the next day.

And that's where the discipline factor comes in. If the market is going against you, you must say to yourself, I'm out, I'm wrong, I'm done, it's kaput. You have to have the self-confidence to be able to step out and make the trade, but you can't allow your ego to overwhelm your judgment.

Q: As you know, there are a lot of traders who are on the sidelines because they went for the home run and just exploded.

Tim: It's discipline. I've been a member of the exchange for 17 years. There are so many guys who could have been great if they had learned that lesson! You see they get caught up in the excitement and emotion—like the public does. They read about a big market move and say, "Geez! You know, I thought that was going to happen. And God! If I was on it, I could have made millions."

But trading is really a business that you have to come and pay attention to every day. There are some days when the opportunities are much greater than on others; but if you're putting the whole thing on the line, eventually you're going to get blown out. That's where the discipline comes in! When I look at my trading, the amount of money that I make or lose in a day is not of great importance to me in evaluating how I traded; what's critical is how my technique was. I mean, I might make 12 trades in a day and lose money on 10 of them and still make money on the day. The reason is I've controlled my risk/reward ratio. If I'm risking $100 to make $1,000, I can be wrong a lot of times and still do well.

Q: Tim, what do you think there is in your background that prepared you for trading?

Tim: Athletics and the family I was raised in. My father was an all-American football player, and he expected, no, demanded, excellence. He never was the typical parent. He didn't say things like, "My son is the greatest," or "My son can't do anything wrong." In today's society, it's always encourage, encourage, encourage! My father took almost the opposite approach. He expected that we would have successes and therefore when we did, even when we received the adulation of the local town or our peers or whatever, he always came down hard on us. He didn't want us to think that this was the end of the road or that our pot of gold was winning the town championship! He made it very clear that there were other goals to achieve. There were other levels to attain; he always emphasized that you can't rest on your laurels. Excellence is a life-long standard!

Q: Can you think of an example?

Tim: I hit a home run in the town championship game and got carried off the field by the other players. It was late in the game, a three-run homer.

Q: How old were you?

Tim: I was 12 years old. My teammates, the other parents, everybody went wild. Earlier in the game, I had struck out. It was the first time I had struck out all year. After the game, in the glow of all this ecstatic celebration my dad just looked at me and said matter of factly, "You struck out in the second inning." I realized, even then, what he was doing. He always tried to get me to focus on how I could improve. He would not allow me the luxury of complacency. I just laughed. I thought to myself, this son-of-a-bitch, he's never going to tell me I'm great, so why worry about it. I'm just going to keep trying my hardest and that'll shut him up!

Q: So was it a valuable lesson?

Tim: It was to me. Here I am 40 years old, and I remember that moment and what I learned from that experience more vividly than I remember hitting the home run.

Q: What did you learn?

Tim: To be the best, you have to work the hardest, you can't just want to be something. You must have the commitment and the discipline. And if you hit a home run yesterday it's irrelevant!

As a trader, you can't say to yourself, hey! I made $300,000 yesterday. I can put $250,000 on the line in the market. In actuality, if you think you're putting $250,000 on the line, it's probably more like $2 million, because something wacky always happens. I was around for Black Monday; I saw things that were truly unbelievable!

Q: Do you think your trading is more of a learned skill or a natural talent?

Tim: In my case, it was definitely learned, because I did not walk onto the trading floor knowing what great trading was all about. I think trading is adaptation. There's no such thing as a great trader forever or for all times. You must adjust to changing conditions. Early on in my career at the NYFE, a vice president in charge of one of the trading desks asked me what I thought of the coffee market. I'd been on the floor for exactly three weeks. I had a commodity chart book but I had never even looked at coffee before. I flipped to the coffee page and said, "It's going limit up!" I was just messing with the guy, you know, playing with his head. So he gets long coffee and wouldn't you know it, coffee goes limit up. He comes back to me the next day and offers me a job to run a trading desk. Remember, all I've been doing at the time is gambling on commodities. I knew nothing!

I'm there trying to learn about the markets and I'm thinking, this guy's a vice president. I'm on Wall Street. Where are all the market wizards? How could this guy be the vice president of anything? I was just messing with him and he thinks I'm a genius: the new market swami! That experience really gave me the confidence to become a trader. I thought, if this guy thinks I'm a genius when I know I'm an idiot, I can really work at this and do all right. It was the most astounding thing to me that this so-called seasoned trader followed me on a trade!

Q: And he's running a Wall Street firm.

Tim: Yeah, and I'm off the beaches of Miami for three weeks, and he wants to pay me $75,000 a year to run his floor operation. At the time I knew how to run a trading desk like I knew how to do open heart surgery—and I didn't go to medical school!

Q: As you look over your trading career, does any trade stand out?

Tim: Yes, right after I started I drew my account down to about $1,500. And really at the time that was all I had—I wasn't disciplined and didn't know what the hell I was doing. The person who was responsible for margins at my clearing firm told me I didn't have enough money in my account to trade.

Q: This was while you were still at the NYFE?

Tim: Yes. However, he said he would allow me to continue to trade as long as I didn't run the account into a debit and traded no larger than a three-contract position. He watched me like a hawk and, I believe, that's where I really learned the discipline. I got the account up to about $10,000. You know, I might make $300 or $400 in a day. I was just chipping away day by day, building the account up in a very rational and disciplined way. After I got the account to over $10,000, I went almost six months before I had a losing day. I built the account up to $1.8 million!

I think the first big losing day that I had I lost $50,000 and I said, "That's it." I walked away from the market and took a few weeks off.

Q: You were still in your 20s; you had made a lot of money in the market. What did it feel like?

Tim: It was great. I had always thought before that if I made a million dollars, I'd retire. Well, I'd been in the business for only seven months and I was over the million-dollar mark. I was hardly thinking of retirement.

Q: You were just ready to get started, right?

Tim: I was ready to stuff more dough in! I mean what's a million? I'm thinking to myself, I've got to make some real money! And the funny thing is, what previously were luxuries, had now become necessities in my life: cars, houses, vacations . . .

If I had to characterize how I spent my early money, I would have to say I spent 90 percent on booze and broads, and the other 10 percent I just pissed away! But quite seriously, I learned a lot from that experience. I was young and lacked discipline. Because of some of the foolish things I did earlier, I'm much more disciplined today.

Q: What do you think is your greatest strength as a trader?

Tim: My ability to just ignore the frenzy. My biggest days are usually wild days. I very rarely get nailed on a volatile day in the market, because my adrenaline's going and I get very focused like I do in athletics. When I get hurt in the market there's not really much going on and I get lulled to sleep. I try to make something of a dull market that's not there.

When the market's fast and furious, I feel like I have a huge advantage over everyone else. I believe it's the same strength that I always had as a player in tight situations in athletics. I can feel my heart pounding. It's almost like a drug when it happens and, interestingly, it makes me incredibly focused and alive!

Q: Like when you would take the last shot?

Tim: Exactly. They call me "Money" on the golf course. Believe me, nobody wants to see me putting against them for money. They know that I'm going to drive a stake into their heart. It's just a surge of energy that I get and I know that I'm not going to miss!

Q: So your strength is that you don't choke?

Tim: Maybe this all relates back to my dad. I can remember as a kid playing Ping-Pong. We'd be rallying. After a 20-shot rally, he'd be laughing, wondering to himself how this eight-year-old is staying with him. I'd see it in his eyes. He couldn't understand why I wasn't choking. He'd try to distract me! He'd ask, "Do you want a bag of apples?" He'd be working me to death trying everything to break my concentration, and nothing would work. I would just keep getting it back, I refused to back off. I took my athletics further than either of my brothers, who are both good athletes, because mentally I was tougher!

Q: And this mental toughness has served you well in the market?

Tim: I don't think that my success has come because I'm a trading genius or because I've got that much better of a trading plan. It all comes down to grace under fire. I don't hesitate when I have to respond. That's my great strength.

Q: What effect has trading had on your marriage?

Tim: It's very difficult. My first marriage didn't last long. I was married for only 14 months. My second marriage has lasted 11 years. In trading, for me, everything is so quick and concise. You're in, you're out; it's black and white. Relationships obviously don't work that way!

When you try to deal with individuals or your wife outside the market in such an absolute way, it doesn't work. It's like a cold slap in the face. "Okay, this is what we're doing!" or "I've made up my mind!" "Can't we discuss this?" No! I spend most of my life making quick decisions that I know are the best routes to arriving at a solution.

Q: How do you keep that in check?

Tim: It's difficult. I'm sure that my wife has a much different view of it. I probably think I've got it more under control than she thinks I do. It's like a scene in the movie *Annie Hall.* Diane Keaton is talking to her psychiatrist who asks about her sex life. She answers, "Oh, doctor, he wants sex all the time. He can't think of anything else. That's all he ever wants!" "Well, how often do you have sex?" he asks and she responds, "All the time, once a week." Then Woody Allen is asked the same question in a separate session and he complains, "We never have sex. She wants nothing to do with it!" "Well, how often do you have it?" he asks and Woody answers, "Practically never, once a week!" So to answer your question, how am I relating to my wife with respect to how the market is affecting us, my view is probably a lot different than hers!

Q: Tim, what has trading taught you about yourself?

Tim: It definitely has taught me a lot about the frailty of the individual. How in the blink of an eye you can be blown out of here! When you experience something like Black Monday with that type of volatility, you realize how nuts this whole thing is. You could get trapped in a position, and can be wiped out before you knew what hit you. That's why I said before trading is all about adaptation. If you don't adapt immediately to a situation like that, you're history. And that's why, as a trader, there's no ironclad set of rules to follow, because in order to be successful you have to change not only to the market but to a variety of situations that are constantly in flux.

It also has taught me something else that really I got from my father but it has been reaffirmed in the market. You need to have discipline and a strong sense of your own moral code, a sense of honor, if you will. This may sound a little overblown, but you also need the personal honesty not to be afraid of the truth.

If I had cancer and was dying, I wouldn't want anybody protecting me from that fact. I wouldn't want someone trying to ease my pain. Just tell me! If you can't handle the truth, that's OK, but I've got to deal with the truth every day of my life and I can't have it whitewashed. What I've learned is that, no matter what, I can handle the truth and I think that gives me a huge advantage in the market.

Q: What do you think distinguishes you from every other trader down on the floor?

Tim: I have my own style. It might look ridiculous at times or maybe it looks like pure genius. You know, on Black Monday I bought the market on the close. I had friends of mine begging me not to do it. They said I was committing suicide. It was, in fact, the greatest buy of all time, and that's exactly why I did it! The other traders were looking at me like I was nuts. I think that the strength of my convictions and intuition about the market is my greatest asset and then the ability to focus when all hell is breaking loose.

My dad used to say what you did yesterday is ancient history. You've got a game today. The score is zero-zero. And the guys you're going up against aren't going to roll over and play dead. The market is so much bigger than anything or anyone that I ever competed against. You have to be prepared and disciplined whenever you walk on the trading floor. You also have to remind yourself that you're just a fly on a rhino's back, and the best you're hoping for is a peaceful ride. If you get swell-headed, the tail's going to get you. The trick is not to end up one dead fly!

CHAPTER 6

Trading Suits Him

Larry Rosenberg

*Mr. Rosenberg is a long-term member of the Chicago Mercantile
Exchange and is a past chairman of its Board of Directors.
He was an active floor trader for many years and continues
to trade successfully for his own account on and off the
exchange floor. He is president of Lake Shore Asset Management
and PMB, an FCM (Futures Commission Merchant).*

Q: What first attracted you to trading?
Larry: I was working my way through school selling men's
clothes, and one of my customers was a big trader. After speaking
with him on a couple of occasions, it just sounded like something
I wanted to do. Also I knew it had to have better potential than
selling suits in a small retail shop.

Q: Your customer was a big trader?
Larry: Lee Stern.

Q: Did he have good taste in suits?
Larry: Yeah, he was all right. He was smart. He let me guide
him!

Q: Well, you've always been a sharp dresser, Larry. So what
happened?
Larry: Lee got me a job as a runner. After being a runner for I
don't know, a year or so, I got drafted. When I got out of the
army, I looked him up again, and I was a little discouraged because the membership prices were moving away from me. When
I went in they were already up to $4,000. I started to save up my

money. By the time I got $1,200 saved, memberships were $7,000. I just couldn't catch up!

So this was 1960 and as I said, I was getting a little discouraged. I had an offer from a company to sell insurance and I was considering taking the job. So I mentioned to someone on the trading floor how I was going to sell insurance. Lee Stern came up to me and said, "Larry, no one wants to sell insurance. Buy a membership!" Fortunately, my mother had a little confidence in me. I borrowed $1,500 and became a Chicago Board of Trade member, but Lee Stern really gave me the kick in the rear.

Q: As you think back, what first attracted you to trading? I mean, Lee Stern is kind of a flashy guy. Was it the lifestyle that attracted you?

Larry: No. Originally I thought I wanted to go to law school but it was more the idea of not working for anybody, creating your own success, just the idea of being judged on your own merits. But really there was also a certain attraction to the traders. There were guys who were just bigger than life.

I can remember one of my first encounters at the Board of Trade as a member. I met a trader by the name of Joe Diamond. Joe was a Georgian, a real big guy, maybe 6 feet 6 inches. He walked around with a ten-gallon hat on. You could tell if he was up or down, because he had this diamond stickpin, and when he was down, he would pawn it, and when he was flush he'd wear it and it would glitter in the pit when he was trading. Joe had made several millions of dollars in the middle and late 50s and then lost it all. I mean today several million dollars is not a lot of money but then it was over the top. And we're sitting at a table, Joe and I, and half a dozen mostly younger guys. And one of them said, "Joe, I don't understand. If you had $5 million, how could you lose it all? Why didn't you just stop when you had a couple left?" And he looked the guy right in the eye, and said with this incredible Georgian twang, "Son, by you asking that question, you ain't ever gonna have $5 million." It's the truth. He was a real piece of work. He used to love to put on what he labeled the Texas spread. He'd just buy limit positions of everything!

Q: This is mostly grains?

Larry: Yeah, in every contract. He was long everything in sight.

Q: So he wouldn't do a traditional hedge buying and selling.

Larry: He'd just buy! You know about 15 years later I heard this saying attributed to one of the Hunt brothers. But I first heard it expressed by Joe Diamond in 1961. "If you know your net worth, you ain't worth much!"

There's another story about Joe Diamond. When he had money in the 50s, he set up trusts. He had a wife and I think if I remember, two kids. He set up the trusts so that if he went broke, his family would be protected. He got hold of a banker and tried to break the trust to get their money. Of course the banker wouldn't do it, fortunately for his family. And until the day he died, Joe used to say, "You can never trust a Yankee banker; they won't even let you use your own money!"

There's one other story about Joe Diamond that is a classic. He wanted to buy a house in Wilmette, right on the lake. Remember we're in the late 50s, and the house was, I don't know, $70,000—something like that.

So Joe's walking around the house with a carpetbag in his hand. Before the Realtor can inform Joe of the asking price, Joe says, "I'll take it." The Realtor says, "Mr. Diamond, don't you want me to tell you the price so that you can counteroffer?" Joe says, "No. If I see something and I like it, I take it." He opened the bag and started to count out the cash!

Q: I heard one like that about a guy that we know who's a big livestock trader from Oklahoma, Eddie Johnson. Apparently he came from a dirt-poor background, and after his first killing in the cattle market he went down to Michigan Avenue and asked for the price on a Rolex President. At the time I think they were selling for $5,500, and he said, "I want that watch." The storekeeper said, "Well, how do you plan to pay for this?" And he said, "I pay for everything in cash," and proceeded to buy 20 of them as Christmas gifts for his relatives.

Larry: I heard the same story.

Q: You know, we hear so much about these kind of traders. We've seen so many of these guys who've come from nothing and have made spectacular fortunes only to lose it all.

Larry: I think that's right. I think Joe said it right: If you're of the mind to stop at a certain point, you're not going to make that kind of fortune.

Q: You've got to go for it all?

Larry: Yes, that is the mind-set of those guys. You've got to go for it all. You never take it off. You're on the pass line all the time. Gene Cashman, a wonderful guy, made a lot of money. The best thing that happened to him was that he was over the limits. The Commodities Futures Trading Commission suspended him. He said that the six months or a year that he was suspended absolutely saved him.

Q: He had a chance to think.

Larry: Exactly!

Q: I would think as with most traders, and certainly with a career that has the longevity of yours, there have to be a lot of ups and downs. Do you think there's anything in your background that prepared you for handling that?

Larry: Well, I think that probably comes from my heritage. My God, my grandparents came here with nothing. It was a very precarious life for them.

Q: The insecurity of it?

Larry: You had to be able to weather whatever life threw at you. My father was a scrap dealer, which was really a way of playing markets, in a much riskier way than I do. He was doing it with real inventory. He had an inventory that he would either sell or be stuck with! So risk taking is in my background on many different levels.

I started by scalping corn and rye. Back in those days, you very rarely had a one-cent range during the entire day, trading eighths. I was doing a lot of spreading in odd lots. It was a tough grind. I had to do other things to supplement my living. I sold clothes three evenings a week and on Saturdays. I clerked at the exchange in the afternoons. I did whatever had to be done so that I could trade and pay my expenses.

I think the guys who have been around for a long time from my generation—that's almost a defining quality of their personalities. They do whatever it takes to succeed in trading and everything else. The successful traders over the years are survivors—you have to be. And you do whatever it takes to survive and sometimes it means getting "real creative"

Q: I heard a story some years ago about a trader who had made a fortune and soon afterward lost it. He had dropped out of high school and so couldn't get a high-paying part-time job. He used to go to O'Hare Airport at night, where he washed floors for $3.50 an hour just to keep himself going. I mean, you hear stories like that among traders, that they do whatever it takes. I think as a group we're really unusual in that respect.

Larry: I think it's the mark of a survivor. The ones who are not tough fall by the wayside. Look down at the bar after the market closes; the ones who won't make it are drinking their brains out!

Q: Can you think of anybody who you knew in your career who stands out as someone who could survive whatever the market threw at him?

Larry: There were a lot of people, really! Rickey Barnes, God, he went up and down. Lee Stern, look at what he went through and much of it not of his own making. These guys are all to be admired, all survivors. I remember years ago Hank Shatkin (of Shatkin Arbor Karlou & Co.) was playing cards and driving a cab at night to supplement his trading. He was a damn good card player!

Look at Pat Arbor. I was the first guy he traded with. Hank Shatkin and I were partners.

Q: You had the clearing firm?

Larry: Yeah, S&R (Shatkin & Rosenberg). I remember when Pat started very well.

Q: I'm sure you do, because he was on your books.

Larry: That's right.

Q: He left for awhile and, as you know, worked on skyscrapers, welding I beams.

Larry: I know I'm a survivor, but when it comes to that, I think that's where I draw the line! I don't think I'd survive that. I get nervous just watching.

Q: That's your instinct for survival!

Larry: That's true.

Q: Larry, what do you think is your greatest strength as a trader?

Larry: Discipline. To be a survivor you must have discipline—without it you're history! I'm a very disciplined person. I always know where I'm getting out. I always know exactly how much I choose to risk!

Q: Having stood next to you on the trading floor, I would say you were great at that. I mean you had the ability to move in and out of positions with great facility.

Larry: Many times in the pit, for example, I would buy some and before I even had it on the card, realize it was the wrong thing to do and I would get out immediately. Obviously, you don't move that quickly off the floor, but it's the same concept. Every time I put a position on, I have my loss point. I might not know exactly where my profit point is, but I know instinctively where I'm wrong.

Q: You know your risk threshold.

Larry: Yeah, exactly. I know where I'm getting out if I'm wrong.

Q: So you believe your greatest strength as a trader is in exercising discipline.

Larry: Absolutely. You know, no one ever busts out of this business losing little bits. It's the one or two biggies that knock you out. Once you protect yourself against that and follow the rules, the rest is pretty vanilla.

Q: Larry, do you think that advice is as true today as it was in 1961?

Larry: I think it was true in 1861 and it will be in 2061. I mean, I think it's a fact of life. That is the life of the trader!

Q: And yet it's so hard for people—not to know it, but to do it!

Larry: That's because of ego, it's having to say you're wrong. If you let your ego get involved, you have no chance, no hope! Once your ego interferes, you're doomed.

I picked up something from an old Chicago Board of Trade guy, Adam Riffel. He had a clearing house. In those days, Adam would come into the soybeans and spread 500, which was a huge number back in the 60s. He was one of the largest traders on the floor.

He would be in and out of hundreds of cars. One day I saw him on the floor and he was trading one lots and I asked him about it. He said something I never forgot: "There's a time when you trade a hundred, and there's a time when you trade just one contract, and you can only trade what the market is telling you is appropriate!" I learned something from Adam Riffel. Many times new traders think that they haven't arrived unless they can do their 10 or 20 or 100 contracts. It's your ego. You must respect what the market is telling you!

Q: Larry, what has been your weakness in trading?

Larry: I think sometimes I'm too conservative.

Q: You don't have that Joe Diamond spirit?

Larry: No, I certainly don't! But sometimes I think I don't let trades fully mature and I get out too early.

Q: Why do you think that is? Is it a fear to lose built-up profit?

Larry: I think part of it is that I'm a product of my environment. And what I mean by that is, being a floor trader for so many years, every night I was even. Settlement price became my statement price in the morning. That's my money, and I don't want to see any of that being given back. On the floor, I might have three losing days in a year. Well, you can't possibly do that in front of a screen.

Q: Larry, what effect do you think trading has had on your personal life and on your marriage?

Larry: I don't really think anything. I was married for many years to my high-school sweetheart, with three kids, and we did it together. I didn't bring the stress home. That's not to say if I lost a lot of money I was real happy, but some of the biggest presents I bought my wife were after a bad day in the market. Anyone can spend money when they're making it; it's when you're losing it . . .

Q: What's the psychology behind that?

Larry: I just think you're showing the world that the loss didn't get you down, and you've still got what it takes, and you have the confidence to come right back. So it was a bad loss, but just a bump in the road. It was a speed bump. And I really think if you let it get to you, it becomes a mountain instead of just a bump along the way.

I've always been pretty good about the emotional side. I never really took it out on anyone in my family. I might not have been real happy, but I never blamed anyone else. You know, it's not the market's fault. It's not the computer's fault. It's not the clearinghouse's fault. It's your fault when you screw up. And ultimately to be successful you must know that. Not read it in a book but live it day in and day out every day you trade.

Q: Of course, the guys who can't assume personal responsibility end up making it somebody else's fault, right?

Larry: Well, that's right. I hear that all the time. "It was the unemployment report!" Hey, that's all part of the game.

Q: Do you think successful traders are different in that respect from other people?

Larry: Well, the really good ones realize that, that they are responsible. I think a lot of traders, though, still haven't learned that, because you hear it all the time.

Q: It was their broker!

Larry: Yeah. Or God, do you believe that lousy fill or my luck or Greenspan said something. And you hear that so often. But you don't hear it from the best traders. I mean, I have never heard people I consider good traders say something like that. Putting responsibility on anyone except for themselves!

Q: Larry, you have been a member of the exchange for over 35 years. You were a major player on the floor. What was your best moment in the market?

Larry: I was chairman of the exchange, and Leo Melamed and I were going to South Africa to develop the gold contract. We went via Rio. But I left the states with a large position in cattle.

There was a report coming out. I got to Rio, and in those days you just didn't pick up the phone and dial. After staying on the phone for what now seems like an eternity, I discovered the market broke sharply the night before the report. I had left like two days earlier and the market fell apart in the last minute of the trade. I was long and my stop was missed by two ticks. The next day the report was released. It was incredibly bullish and the market was up the limit three days in a row. It was the biggest trade I ever had in the market!

I just knew if I was standing in that pit, there was no way I'm going to sit through that kind of break going into a report on the close. I'm gone!

Q: So you ended up capturing the whole move in the market.

Larry: The whole move, and added to it. I was ecstatic. It was one of the biggest trading highs of my career. I mean, here I am down in Rio and Leo and I were working very hard!

Q: You're winking. You and Leo must have been working very hard in Ipanema!

Can you describe what it feels like when you are going through a period like that when every one of your ships seems to be coming in?

Larry: Yeah, you really feel like you're bulletproof. The market breaks, you buy it and it goes up. The market goes up, you sell it and it breaks. You seem to be completely in sync. You just get in a rhythm with the market. You're in perfect tune with whatever's happening. I'm not really sure what creates that, but as long as you've got it, you must go with it!

Q: What was the lowest moment you've had in the market?

Larry: Oh, boy, I've had a few of those, I'll tell you!

Q: Only a few? You're lucky!

Larry: Early on in my career Hank and I had some money problems but I can't think of a specific incident like the cattle trade when I was in Rio. But there are periods where my trading experiences lapses. Things aren't going well and you push even more. Usually if I have a losing streak, I'll take time off. I mean when I say "take time off," I have compounded a losing streak by making the mistake of going away with positions. Now I just mean take time off. No position!

Q: So you're totally out of the market.

Larry: Totally. I don't call, I don't do anything. I come back and start fresh all over again.

Q: Do you go any place special?

Larry: I like to go down to the Caribbean and swim. I used to ski, really anything to clear my head out so I can start again with a bright outlook.

I'll tell you a funny story. I promise you this is a true story. About ten years ago I was having a dry spell. I was sitting in the members' lounge having a cup of coffee with a guy and he says to me, "Well, how is it going?" I said, "Not great." He said, "I'm trading low too," and he asked, "Why don't we take a few days off?" So that afternoon we're at O'Hare heading for a plane for Los Angeles. We arrive four hours later a little tipsy. We had a couple of drinks along the way.

The next day, we're "working" you know, we're all decked out, silk shirts, sunglasses, the whole thing—like the two wild and crazy guys from Saturday Night Live!

Well, this particular guy, who I should add is slightly cheaper than Jack Benny, and I are walking down Rodeo Drive and he spots this store that he wants to go into, Hermès. He never heard of it and is attracted by a silk robe that is displayed in the window. He turns to me and says, "That's a great-looking robe." And he says to the saleslady, "I'll take two—one for me and one for my friend." He has no idea of the prices at Hermès. I mean he is really just into the moment. I said to him, "Hey, you don't have to."

He says, "Get out of here. Friends!" He looks at the bill, $4,000 and goes from being flushed from too many drinks to stone-cold white. I ask, "What's the problem?" He literally couldn't talk; his mouth was wide open like a cartoon character. Finally he blurted out "Well, maybe my friend doesn't want one!"

Q: Did you?

Larry: Yes. Sure I did, but it was OK. I was having enough fun just watching him sweat.

Q: But he did take one robe?

Larry: Yeah, he was too embarrassed not to take one of them. I think the poor guy walked around with that large Hermès box for the rest of the weekend. You know, every time I see him, I ask him about the robe!

Q: I've bought cars that cost less than that robe.

Larry: When I was chairman of the board, I went to Europe for the Chicago Mercantile Exchange to develop business.

Q: You were doing promotional work for the exchange?

Larry: Exactly, and we'd give press conferences, and at the time there were more of us than there were reporters. Before I left, a friend of mine said, "Geez. If you're going to be traveling to

Europe for the exchange, you ought to get a suit made of this new fabric. It's great. It doesn't wrinkle."

Q: Polyester?

Larry: Exactly right. It made sense to me! So I buy this suit. A beautiful blue pinstripe, polyester. I didn't pay much attention, packed it and left for London. The first time I put it on, it didn't feel right. I looked in the mirror and said, "I'll go out in shorts before I wear this in public." I threw it in the closet. I think it may still be in London!

Q: And it was expensive polyester also, right?

Larry: Nothing but the best. You know, I have an aversion to that stuff? Even when I was playing golf, I wouldn't wear polyester golf slacks. I wouldn't wear anything with polyester.

Q: Do you think traders feel more alive than other people?

Larry: Absolutely. If you're trading, you've got to be alive. I mean, every day is a new day. You know, you control your own destiny.

Q: Physically too. I think we all feel energized.

Larry: I think so, and even when I get beat up, that's why I take off, to get reenergized. One of the reasons why I left the floor is because it no longer energized me. After 30 years on the floor, I felt burned out. I love trading upstairs. Now I'm reenergized. I enjoy life!

Q: After 35 years of doing this day in and day out, what has trading taught you about yourself?

Larry: It has taught me I'm not as smart as I thought I was.

Q: Well, they say the market can be very humbling.

Larry: That's for sure! This is the only business in the world where a guy with a 160 IQ can go broke, and a guy with an 80 IQ can make $10 million! In fact, sometimes I think the 80 IQ has got a better shot at it; he has no fear!

Q: But ultimately, Larry, you know very well it is the guys with the higher IQ who . . .

Larry: Well, I read somewhere that traders as a group had high IQs. I don't know if that's true or not. I could fill up this trading room with a lot of people who could disprove that fact. But let's face it: You've got to pay the price. There's no free education. When you go to school, you pay tuition, and that's just what you're doing in the market. I don't think you ever learn anything that's free. Either you learn from your mistakes or you're doomed to repeat them.

I think coming off the floor has been very important for me. I really do enjoy it. It has given a whole new life to me. I feel for me, it has been like starting a whole new business.

Q: Larry, what do you think distinguishes you from all the other traders?

Larry: I think there are a couple of things. We spoke about them before. One is discipline. And two is a sense of self, being secure. I'm very happy with who and what I am. You know, I guess we all make changes, and there's certainly no perfection, but I'm very happy with my life. I'm also committed to learning something new every day.

Q: Did you learn something today?

Larry: Yeah.

Q: After 35 years, what did you learn today?

Larry: It's a little technical thing. It works pretty well. I just kept watching my indicators and I picked up something today. I took a trade using it and it worked out pretty well.

Q: One more day to survive.

Larry: That's right. But you know what? These things are good for you psychologically, because you always are there to learn something new. It's reenergizing to operate with that attitude.

Q: New day, new beginning.

Larry: That's right, and to know that when the bell rings tomorrow, I'll be here.

Q: You'll be right where you are right now.

Larry: Right! Ready to go!

CHAPTER 7

Tennis Anyone?

William H. "Toby" Crabel

Mr. Crabel is a long-term trader and market analyst. He has been a floor trader and wrote a newsletter that market professionals closely followed. Mr. Crabel has done extensive computer testing of short-term price patterns and is the author of the book Day Trading with Short-Term Price Patterns and Opening Range Breakout *(1989). He is currently a commodities trading adviser, managing over $50 million.*

Q: Toby, what first attracted you to trading?

Toby: I was a three-time all-american in tennis. I wanted to be a professional but I was not at the very top. I discovered commodity trading and found it very exciting. Only later did I realize that that aspect of trading is both positive and negative. Psychologically speaking, the excitement can be motivating but also very debilitating.

Q: What was your trading like at the very beginning?

Toby: The markets were fantastic. There were huge, dramatic swings both up and down. I remember buying T-bills in 1981 and then watching them go limit up for three days in a row. That doesn't happen anymore! Or selling gold and having it break $36 in a half hour. Unfortunately, that frenzy of activity created expectations that could not be fulfilled. It was just an unbelievable trading period! And I got really caught up in just the electricity and emotion of the market. I also had this tremendous fascination with the trading floor. You would get this feeling that something big was happening here!

Q: When you started, were you trading on the exchange floor?

Toby: I started as a runner. I was working on the floor for a large local in the cattle pit, Tim Brennan. He needed someone to handle the charts and I filled that need for him. Then I moved upstairs and sat in front of a screen where I followed a lot of different markets. I didn't really know anything at that point, but I began to learn a few technical points, all pretty basic stuff. I discovered that as much as I liked the floor, there still was enough satisfaction trading from upstairs.

Q: How were you doing during this period?

Toby: I was volatile. I made money for Tim trading his accounts and I made money for clients. But as I said I had a lot of volatility. There are so many stories like this in commodities! You take $10,000, run it up to $100,000 and then you lose most, or all of it, shortly thereafter. Personally, I tended to have a lot of fear so that I tried to keep the money I made.

Q: Toby, does trading still have the same attraction for you today that it did initially?

Toby: It's more of a business now. The initial infatuation and excitement doesn't exist for me anymore. It is an issue that I've really had to deal with. The course that I've taken is a much more methodical approach to the markets. I think if I stayed in it for the excitement, I could only trade on a very small scale. Of course, when I say excitement I mean the emotional charge that you get from swift market movements and big profits—that kind of thing. I should add that I still do get excited about trading, but it's different today. The excitement comes from seeing my management business succeed.

Q: Growing your business?

Toby: Yes, and realizing the control that I'm able to display. There's a deep feeling of satisfaction that I derive from conducting my business and managing my life in a rational manner.

Q: Toby, you've really been able to achieve something that very few traders have been able to accomplish. You have consistent, positive trading results with almost no volatility. There aren't too many traders who can do it.

Toby: That has been my goal. It's what I value and is the hardest thing to accomplish in this business. I've impressed myself with what is possible. But you know, there's still a lot of work to be done!

Q: Can you talk a little bit about what the process has been like?

Toby: It's been a long and difficult process. There were times when I made more money than I thought at all possible, when the dollars just sort of fell in my lap. There were times when I couldn't even sleep at night because I was just so excited. When I lost money, I was just terribly depressed. It had a huge effect on me. So the emotion really was affecting me whether I made or lost!

Early in 1987 I had a four-month drawdown that really set me back. I questioned whether I even wanted to trade at that point. I took a year to reevaluate the whole thing. That's when I wrote my book, *Day Trading with Short-Term Price Patterns and Opening Range Breakout.* It was a great time for personal reflection.

I realized that what I love about trading is the intellectual challenge of the business. And I decided that I could never leave. I wanted to be involved in it and I knew it was something I could do very well. So I regrouped, came back to Chicago, and started writing a market letter that I sold to floor traders. Then in 1990 I ran into another drawdown. And that was it for me! The moment of truth. In 1987, I was committed to figuring out what it would take to create a proper program to run a business as a professional trader. The thing that I learned very clearly in 1990 was that the volatility had to drop dramatically so that I could control the risk. By 1992 I had some of the mechanisms in place. Unfortunately, it wasn't quite as systematic as they are today. But the thinking process was there.

In reality, the answer was completely moving away from discretionary trading to the point where I am today. I am completely systematic in my approach. It was hard to give up the discretion!

Actually it took me until early 1995 to finally become comfortable with something that I thought was better than what I could do on a discretionary basis. It was developing the systematic approach which allowed me to eliminate the volatility: the emotional volatility and the uneven trading performance.

Q: Toby, how would you characterize your tennis game?

Toby: I was an extremely conservative tennis player. When I was playing my best, I tended not to miss. I would just keep hitting the ball back, always keeping it in play!

Q: So it was consistency, rather than the big shot?

Toby: Yeah. I've done some work with myself on this very point, on certain insecurities that I had growing up as a result of an erratic family life. I am always searching for security and consistency. Volatility is something that I just can't stand in a business or in any other part of my life.

Q: I guess, Toby, if you're searching for security and consistency in your life, commodities seems like the obvious choice!

Toby: Well, that's very interesting. This comes back to the dichotomy in my trading approach before I eliminated the emotion. I was honestly searching for security. I thought I could have discretion and low volatility. I can't have both—I really can't! For me that means, as I said before, operating a secure business.

Q: This approach of eliminating the emotion really grew out of your natural desire for security and an aversion to risk. It was reflected in your tennis game. Is that correct?

Toby: Right. These are inherently exciting professions that are prone to stimulating fears and insecurities!

Q: And you were able to get the security and excitement by figuring out a way to manage the risks!

Toby: That's true. In tennis, as I matured in my game, I felt very confident in what I did. The longer I was engaged in tennis, the more I thought about it. This applies to trading. Also, I feel that the confidence allows me to maintain control. Right now I feel very confident and very much in control, and I'd like to keep it that way. I believe I can conduct my business at this point better than I ever have. I know how to keep the ball inside the lines!

Q: Do you think that for you trading was more of a learned skill or a natural talent?

Toby: I don't think there is such a thing over the long run as natural talent in trading. You know, there are people like Paul Tudor Jones, but he came from a tremendous trading background. I think his uncle was a cotton trader with whom he studied. He also worked with professional cash traders in New Orleans before he traded on the cotton exchange. So he had years of experience before he became a money manager. I don't believe in natural talent! I think this whole thing is all about perspiration. The idea of natural talent, I think, is way overblown. The markets are unforgiving. I think you have to learn what's right; otherwise, you're not going to survive. When you come out of the womb, you don't have anything particularly natural that's going to allow you to survive in the outside environment. You have to learn what life requires. There are so many complexities that are involved in being a successful trader. I can't think of anything innate or instinctual about it. I think, as I said a moment ago, it's about perspiration, hard work, and discipline. The fact that inherently someone may have a little bit more adrenaline flowing in their system than someone else is not relevant! That's not the quality that is important for success in this business!

Q: What do you think is your greatest strength as a trader?

Toby: Well, there are a couple: perseverance and really giving myself enough time to learn what I need to know. I've been extremely forgiving and patient with myself, considering the difficulties that I've encountered.

The way I've approached trading has been very consistent with the way I approached tennis. I've always been very disciplined about my method of gaining knowledge. I was extremely diligent when it came to practice. I practiced almost obsessively. I practiced much more than anybody else that I knew. I wish I had had the focus and the understanding of my own psychology that I have developed in trading as a tennis player. I think I would have been a much stronger competitor. But I also know that as you look back you always kind of think, gee, how much better I could have done with the knowledge and the wisdom that I have now! So maybe youth is wasted on the young!

Q: What effect has trading had on your marriage?

Toby: That's a good question. My wife and I have had a lot of changes in our marriage. We tended to change in the same direction at the same time, which is fortunate. Lori and I could have easily gone separate ways, but the changes in our lives brought us closer together. We cared enough about each other to listen and we tended to agree with one another. It has been an interesting phenomenon. We have made a lot of changes and some that were fundamental ones.

Basically we came out of the 60s. We were sort of hip and wanted to explore different ways of life. We traveled in Europe and came back to the United States, and then studied different philosophies and religious practices. We got involved with some things that later we both agreed were wrong.

Q: What was it that you felt was wrong?

Toby: In broad terms, it was another perspective on living. It was a pretty involved and intense thing. We found that it wasn't right for us. It was really easy to figure out too because all you had to do was open your eyes!

Q: Was it a cult?

Toby: Not exactly. It was kind of a Hindu derivative. We did some meditation. On the surface it had real appeal because we were trying to find some unity in our lives. I had just come off the professional tennis circuit and Lori and I had traveled together and it was very stressful and we were looking to calm down.

Q: The search for security minus emotional volatility?

Toby: Sure. In 1987, when I went through my year of reevaluation, I decided it just wasn't right. Since then, I've looked at things from what I think is a much clearer perspective.

Paradoxically and interestingly, it was trading, not Eastern meditation, that gave me the answers I was looking for. You see, I thought I would find the security I needed in Eastern philosophy. I thought it was going to ground me and center me, that it would make me a little better at what I did. But it is trading that has given me a philosophical direction. In order to improve my trading I had to assess reality accurately.

I was constantly putting myself on the line. I was really working at something, I had all these emotional responses that I had to deal with and learn from. I learned about fear and courage and personal honesty. All the internal questions that come to the surface cry out for answers!

I mean, the contrast between working and meditating, sitting in a chair all day and doing nothing. There's nothing about life there! Pursuing a career in trading is the antithesis of that experience. I found the other approach debilitating. It was taking me in the wrong direction.

I would like to make one thing clear. It is not that trading replaced religion for me, because obviously trading is not a philosophy, but it pointed me and my wife in a direction where philosophically we essentially dropped mysticism and chose to look at the world square in the eye. We were forced to be objective.

Q: Toby, what specifically has trading taught you about yourself?

Toby: Well, there are a lot of things. Ask me what are my best qualities and I learned them as a result of my trading experiences.

Q: The ability to persevere and be patient?

Toby: Yes, one thing my career really proves is that I really stick to it until I get it right.

Q: That sounds like something that's always been part of your personality.

Toby: Yes. It certainly was true of my tennis. I wouldn't stop practicing until I was hitting just so. And then I'd practice some more.

Let's face it, there have been tough times. I've questioned whether I was cut out to be a trader, but I've also been fortunate. I mean, there are a million ways that you can trip yourself up in this business. What I've always been willing to do is find a new way that works and is consistent.

Q: What do you think distinguishes Toby Crabel from everyone else?

Toby: Well, my wife put it well. She said I'm not flashy but I'm solid. You know what people used to say about me in tennis. They couldn't imagine I was a good tennis player because they thought I "looked slow." But they'd watch me for a little while and realize I was getting to every ball. Wherever it was hit I would return it, and I could hit it back pretty damn well! The same thing is true of my trading. If people look at my trading record, initially all they see is the relatively low returns. They'll say "He's OK, not very flashy." But, if they look long enough, they're probably going to see one of the best return to risk ratios in the business. In other words, anyone who "really" looks at me will see some real substance.

CHAPTER 8

Hook, Line, and Sinker

Dennis Weinmann

*Mr. Weinmann is a principal and founder of Coquest, Inc.,
a registered commodity trading adviser and
commodity pool operator.*

Q: What first attracted you to trading?

Dennis: I was introduced to the stock market at an early age. When I was 13 I was given some shares in a high-school textbook publishing company called Johnson's Publications. At the time, I didn't think much of it, but once I started receiving dividend checks I just thought that this was the greatest thing in the world, that they'd pay me to hold this stock.

Q: How big of a check was it?

Dennis: Oh, it wasn't that big. Maybe $20 a quarter. But when I was 13 years old, 20 bucks would go a long way.

Q: Did you spend the money or did you save it?

Dennis: My brother was the spender and I was the saver. He'd go out and spend it all and I'd save it and loan it to him at interest.

Q: Did he pay it?

Dennis: Sure! I always loved making money off of my money. I found that very interesting! So, as I was saying, I had an early attraction to the stock market. I dabbled in it through high school, just buying and selling small stocks. When I got into college, I ran a bunch of businesses and made a decent amount of money, which allowed me to get more and more into the stock market.

Q: What did you study at college?

Dennis: I studied economics at the State University of New York at Oneonta, because it was what I was good at. Originally, I wanted to be an accountant.

Q: So how did you start trading?

Dennis: While I was at school I had a little more money, so I was trading. In the summer I was a sailing instructor at a yacht club. My mother had just recently gotten remarried and I think in an effort by her husband to kind of befriend me, he asked me what I wanted to do when I graduated. I had no idea, of course. So I said, "I don't know." He said he had a very successful client who would be more than happy to talk to me about trading commodities. So I said, "Okay." I called him up and he invited me down to the exchange. He took me around the floor of the New York Mercantile Exchange and I just thought it was the greatest thing since sliced bread. I could not believe that people did this for a living!

Q: Dennis, what did you think was so great about it?

Dennis: The excitement! Just what seemed to me at that time to be complete chaos, and how much money was changing hands—the hundreds of billions of dollars that were moving back and forth and how it all seemed to work out at the end of the day. I think even more so than Chicago, New York trading looks very chaotic.

I'm a big fan of New York exchanges. I know a lot of people in Chicago aren't! I think Chicago probably has the best exchange out there. But I really do think that New York does a pretty good job with a limited amount of space.

Q: Did you actually trade on the floor in New York?

Dennis: The guy I was telling you about, Jerry Rafferty, owned a floor brokerage group. At the time it was probably one of the three largest floor brokerage groups in the crude oil market. Jerry offered me a job. I think he offered me a job, A, because he liked my stepdad and, B, because I was a sailing instructor and he wanted to learn how to sail. So Jerry asked, "Well, when do you start?" I said, "July 1st." And he asked, "Well, when do you get out of school?" and it was like, May 7th. And he said, "Well, work on the floor, start right away. If you like it, you can stay; if not, just let me know. Just give me a couple of days' notice." So a few days later I started and I loved it. And within four weeks, I was Jerry's right-hand clerk. At the time, he was one of the largest locals on the floor in the New York market. You know, crude oil was becoming a pretty big contract: heating oil was there, gasoline was there. This was right before they switched from leaded gasoline to unleaded gasoline. So you know, that was back in 1986 and I just loved it and I thought this was just great! That's what got me hooked. Having worked down there and seeing really young guys making a lot of money.

Q: Were you filling orders in the ring?

Dennis: No. I was Jerry's right-hand clerk. I worked the phones for awhile, taking orders and tracking positions and doing stuff like that.

Q: So you actually never traded on the floor but did what you were doing give you a sense of excitement and vitality of the market?

Dennis: Right. There's a way you can work on the floor and not pick up anything and then you can be like me and work on the floor and pick up everything! I was like a sponge. I asked a lot of questions; I knew who were the good traders, and I watched them very closely.

Q: How could you tell who were the good traders?

Dennis: The people who were making the most money were the good traders in my eyes!

Q: How could you tell?

Dennis: You knew who the guys were because you'd see what kind of cars they drove. Obviously, it's a small community down there and the most successful traders stood out!

Q: Could you identify anything specific that they were doing in the market?

Dennis: At first, I couldn't. Basically, what it taught me and what I'll still tell you today is that you can make money trading a whole lot of different ways. Even down on the trading floor people trade differently. I had a friend who was strictly a back-month spread trader. I had another friend who would strictly trade positions. A lot of guys I knew just scalped. Everyone did something different but they all made good money!

Q: So what first attracted you to trading was the incredible vitality of the floor, the huge exchange of money, and the electricity of being in the market. Is that correct?

Dennis: I would say yes. I went hook, line, and sinker for this business. You know, it's like my whole life I dreamed of playing a pro sport. I think trading is the closest thing to sports that I could ever find.

Q: Which sport did you dream of playing?

Dennis: I'd play any of them. When you're an athlete your whole life, you always dream of being a pro playing in the big game! I was never good enough at any of them but, God, I loved playing them all.

Q: So trading is the closest thing to being in the big game?

Dennis: I would say so. It's a bigger game in my opinion. And you know, that's why a lot of athletes become traders. I know, for instance, [former Chicago Bear] Matt Suhey traded in Chicago and Callahan from the 1980 U.S. hockey team did as well. I think trading and professional sports are very similar.

Q: Now that you've been at it for awhile, does trading still hold the same attraction for you?

Dennis: Oh, yeah. I love what I do! And I'll tell you that makes it a whole lot easier because it isn't easy being a trader. It's extremely emotionally draining. And if I didn't love it, I don't think I'd be successful!

Q: What is it about trading that you love so much?

Dennis: Every day is a new day and you have a bottom line. It's your scorecard. And whether you choose to keep score on a daily, weekly, or monthly basis, every day you know exactly where you stand and that's your bottom line. That's your equity.

Q: Do you think anything in your background prepared you for trading?

Dennis: Well, I grew up in New York City, in Queens, in what I consider a middle-class neighborhood.

I was dyslexic and I had a lot of trouble in public schools. So I went to private school to try to help my dyslexia and basically what it did was promote my troublemaking. I was a rowdy child. I was extremely hyperactive, full of energy. In retrospect, I think I was never fully challenged in school. I kind of took it out on the teachers. I was just bored all the time. So I was thought to be kind of a troublemaker.

Q: What effect do you think this experience has had on your trading?

Dennis: I grew up street-smart and I think that helps. You know, I'm not saying I'm not real smart. I did very well in college. Having street smarts, using common sense, knowing which battles to fight and knowing which ones to walk away from, was just something that you know every day growing up in New York City. I went to Cardova High School, which was a tough school. We had two full-time New York City cops monitoring the halls. And, you know, there could be trouble if you walked around the wrong corner. Knowing which fight to stand up to, and which ones to walk away from, is I think a pretty good analogy for trading the market. Knowing when to stop yourself out and knowing when to hang on a little longer, looking for the market to come back.

Q: Did you ever stand up to fight when you should have walked away from the market?

Dennis: October 1987!

Q: What happened?

Dennis: I was trading a ton of stocks and I had built a very large nest egg at a young age. I made a lot of money in the stock market! The nice thing was I didn't care about the money, which made it easier for me to trade. I never got consumed with having the money. I just loved making it! I didn't need to live on it. I had the same life standard whether I had money or not. So having money in the bank was just a way of keeping score. I liked making the money, that is what I enjoyed. So I just kept trading and I made and made and made, and then came October of 1987 and I lost everything—and more!

Q: What was it like for you and what did you learn from that experience?

Dennis: The best thing that I learned and I'm still learning is that a trader who isn't continually learning new things about himself isn't a trader. It's my job to keep learning about myself and the market. You've got to continually learn new things and adapt!

And the second you stop, and you say this is the way I'm going to trade from now on and you don't keep an open mind, the market will beat you.

Q: Dennis, when you were making money, how did you spend it?

Dennis: Mostly on traveling. I'd travel to Chicago for the weekend, or I'd go to Florida, California, or Vegas. If I felt like it, I'd go skiing in Colorado. I loved to travel. And I was spending it going out on dates. I mean, I was trading it mostly. I wasn't spending it foolishly. I wasn't consumed with the fact that I had money.

Q: Right. But you got caught in the electricity of making the money, right?

Dennis: Right, making it. But I didn't lose my money because I was stupid spending it. I lost my money because I was stupid trading it!

Q: Let's talk about that. What happened to you in the crash?
Dennis: The funny thing was at the time I was becoming a student of technical analysis more and more. I was working with someone I considered to be one of the better technicians in our industry, someone who very few people even know about. You know, a lot of the good people in this industry are unknown because they sit in an office and make a lot of money trading! They don't want to be known! This gentleman was a great technician. We were watching the market together before the crash and he goes, God, we got sell signals in the Dow. It looks like it wants to come off. I said, yeah, it really looks weak. And he said, "Dennis, get out of all your stocks." And I said, "No, my stocks aren't affected by the Dow." I mean, I literally said that. I was so caught up in the fact that I was a good stock picker that I refused to let a short-term correction in the Dow stand in my way. In reality, I wasn't such a good stock picker. I was in the greatest bull market of our time! And you know, you could throw a dart at any stock and it would have gone up. Well I was buying all the ones that you heard about. I was long the Liz Claibornes and Prime Computer and Atari and Nike and Reebok and all the big stocks that everyone knew about. They just kept going up!

Q: As my partner says, nothing will make you a genius like a good bull market!

Dennis: Exactly. And I'll tell you what, when I was in my 20s I believed my own bullshit. I really thought I was good. And then the crash came and I lost everything. I sat there and I watched the market drop and I just watched it with disbelief. I was in awe of how dramatically a market could move.

Q: Right. I was on the floor of the exchange the day of the crash so I kind of saw it up close. And for anybody who experienced it, it really was something. I mean, you really witnessed financial meltdown occurring all around you. I would say without question it was the single most significant experience I've had in all my years of trading.

Dennis: Mine too!

Q: But to get back to your experience. So here you are, still in your 20s, you've made a lot of money, then lost it, which as you know now is a fairly common experience. How did you come back?

Dennis: I started talking to people I really respected. I called an economics professor of mine who had been my mentor through college. I talked to my mother and I talked to some successful traders on the floor. And basically what I realized was I was a young guy who was broke and that everyone else I knew was basically broke, so that wasn't too bad. I still had a job, which was good, and I had just learned an incredibly valuable lesson that I couldn't have learned had I gone to Harvard for 50 years! I learned about markets. From that day on I gained a respect for markets. Had that not happened to me at such a young age, done such damage to me financially, I don't think I would have respected markets nearly as much. I know I respect the market immensely and I know that the reason that I respect the market is because of what I learned in 1987.

Q: What do you think is your greatest strength as a trader?

Dennis: I think my greatest strength is my patience and my ability to hold onto a winner. I don't know that anyone is willing or able to stay with a winner as long as I am. I will literally hold it forever if it doesn't go against me. I have no desire to take profits if the market is going my way.

Q: How do you define whether it's going in your favor or not?

Dennis: Obviously, at different times in a trade you define it differently. In general, as long as we make new highs—you know, higher highs and higher lows everyday, and as long as we stay above key support. If we're settling in the top 25 percent of the day's range. I look at a lot of different things. But the key point is, I'm willing to hold the winner forever until the market tells me to get out.

I think my other strength as a trader is patience. I never feel like I'm in a rush. I also have the ability to honestly believe that if I make a thousand trades I'll be up! So I look at every trade as one tenth of 1 percent of my next thousand trades. And so, emotionally, I really don't let any individual trade bother me. I can lose and that's not a problem. I just continue to be disciplined. I know that if I do these trades continually, I will make money.

Q: You mentioned earlier that you were a sailing instructor. Did you sail competitively?

Dennis: Yes, I did.

Q: Do you think sailing has affected your trading in any way?

Dennis: Yes. I use sailing analogies a lot. A lot of the things in life that I enjoy are similar. I enjoy sailing, I enjoy skiing, I enjoy golf, I love trading! What is it about racing sailboats competitively that's so similar to trading? The best sailors in the world don't win every race! The best sailors lose races sometimes. That doesn't make bad sailors. Having a losing trade doesn't make you a bad trader and it doesn't necessarily make you wrong. I think so many people get caught up in each individual trade! The way I analyze markets I don't say I'm 100 percent sure that the market is going higher. I say I think we've got a 60 percent shot that I'm going to be right. That's a great opportunity for me. I make 100 trades, I'm going to be wrong 40 times, that's still no big deal, okay. So I don't look at losing trades as bad trades, and I don't look at losing trades as being wrong. I look at losing trades as representing the 40 times out of a 100 that I had to trade to ultimately be successful. I try to look at it that way. When I raced sailboats, I enjoyed it because we won more than we lost and we were successful at it. But we lost many times. We tended to be better light-air sailors than heavy-air sailors! There are people who tend to trade markets better in trading ranges than in trends. The focus has to be on the process rather than any individual trade.

Q: Do you think for you trading is more of a learned skill or a natural talent?

Dennis: I think there are people who are born with the ability to become good traders and there are people who enhance that ability and become great traders. I think it's something that can be taught. But I think that to be truly good, to be an excellent trader, to be a market wizard, you have to have some inbred talent or personality trait that allows you to develop that skill.

Q: I remember reading in a profile of you in a trading magazine that in your opinion trading is an art form. What did you mean by that?

Dennis: So many people want to turn trading into a science. When the moving average crosses here and we violate it by X percentage, you buy, you put your stop this percentage here, and you hold until there. So many people think there are definitive answers to trading. They think there's got to be a computer program that knows what all markets are going to do next. There's got to be a way to develop some kind of systematic approach that's going to make you barrels of money.

Q: And you disagree with that point of view?

Dennis: One hundred percent. There is no answer. There are just a bunch of questions!

Q: So that's where the art comes in? Being able to address the questions in a creative or intuitive way?

Dennis: Creative and intuitive, yes. Understanding that there's not an answer! Let me use another analogy from sports. The greatest golfer in the world, Jack Nicklaus, at one time didn't win every tournament. This is what I think is so interesting. He still had a coach to teach him how to swing better, even though no one had a better swing than him! Let's say that no one has a better swing than Tiger Woods now. But he still has a coach. And that tells me there's no such thing as perfection in any of these things. Of course, there's the goal to strive closer and closer toward it. But I think one of the attractions of trading is that you can always get better. And therefore, I never get bored. I always think I can get myself to a higher level.

Q: Do you think that traders are different from most people?

Dennis: Absolutely. If they're not, they're not good traders. You just naturally look at things differently. Let me give you an example of how I think about things. I'll walk into a car dealership and say, I wish I could go short these cars and buy them back once they get into the parking lot. I live my life as a trader. I don't have insurance on my car other than minimum liability because I'm not willing to buy some out of the money options from someone else!

All I have is what I'm required to by law. And other than that, I don't want it. Health insurance, I have a very high deductible and I'm willing to take that risk of a high deductible so that my payments are lower. Okay, most people say I'm a nut! I say insurance companies are selling me an overpriced option and they're making money over time on me. I don't want it! I want to be a seller of that option, not a buyer, and so I'm not willing to play their game.

Q: Dennis, what was your best moment in the market?

Dennis: Not a fair question. My best moment is when I'm in sync with the market and feeling alive.

Q: That's a good answer.

Dennis: I mean, usually people would say I made 20 grand, 30 grand, 80 grand in a day. Bullshit! I don't go home the day I make large sums of money any happier than the day that I lost money. There are days when I'm frustrated because I think I might have done something incorrectly, but I learn from that. And there are days I go home where I say, "Yeah, you know, I was dead right. We kicked it, because our timing was really good." I might say, "Yeah, I really stomped the market well this time because my entry was really nice." So it is a case of everything clicking. But I don't look at trading as any individual bet.

Being a successful trader, in my opinion, isn't an exciting living. It's not one big day, it's a lot of little things adding up. It's lose 100, lose 200, win 300, lose 50, win 100, lose 50. I love what I do. When I go to bed on Sunday night, I have a smile on my face because I'm pumped to go to work on Monday. Yeah, I enjoy life and I'm alive because I like my job. I think other people who like their jobs are equally as alive. I mean, I have a good friend, a very close friend who is a schoolteacher and who really believes that she makes a difference in this world by the way that she teaches. And she's really alive and loves her work and is excited about teaching. I think that's the way I feel about trading. It's very important that you enjoy what you do.

Q: What do you think trading has taught you about yourself?

Dennis: If you do not respect these markets, they will eat you up and spit you out. And it's not personal, it's just the way it works. I think trading is a maturing process. I think it happens to speed it up because there's money involved and it just makes you look at yourself. The market also humbles you. It has taught me to live my life on an even keel. I try to walk a straight line and I don't take my work home with me.

Q: Dennis, what do you think distinguishes you from other traders?

Dennis: A lot of things. Do I think I'm the best trader in the world? I don't think so. Do I think I have the ability to be pretty damn close? Yes, I do. You know what distinguishes me from all the others? I think differently than a lot of traders. I tend to have a unique point of view. And I think that distinguishes me. Analysis-wise, do I look at stuff that's so much different than everyone else? No! I think a lot of people are astonished when they see what some of the really good traders look at. I don't think it needs to be rocket science to make you money. I think a lot of locals prove that every day. Locals trade and make money and have no idea where the market is going. And a lot of them don't do any technical analysis. They trade the market. They watch the market. They buy when they think it looks good and they sell it when it looks bad. That's not analysis. That's an art form. That's trading in the true sense where you are trading the swings in the market. So, to get back to your question, what makes me different is my approach. It's different in that none of my ideas have been codified. Nothing I'm saying is earth breaking. It's the way in which I use my personality and bring it to the market place. If I told you everything I did in my trading and you sat next to me and did the same thing, you'd still trade differently than me cause we're different people! And so what makes me different is the way that my personality interacts with the market.

Q: Dennis, are you saying that your trading really is no more than a vehicle for you to express yourself and your personality?

Dennis: Exactly. And to me, that's essential. I think a lot of people say, "Help me become a better trader." And I'm saying, well I can tell you what things you need to do and what things you need to eliminate. But I can't make you a good trader, because only you can do that if it's consistent with your personality.

CHAPTER 9

Seeing Is Believing

David M. Gordon

*Mr. Gordon is an independent equities trader
residing in Los Angeles, California.*

Q: David, what first attracted you to trading?

David: I started trading when I was about 11 years old. I remember picking up this strange ability of finding the stock pages in the newspaper. Back then, the *Los Angeles Times* included the quotes with the sports section and I'd be able to open the whole newspaper, which was delivered folded twice and tied, right to the business pages. From the time I was a kid it was the part of the paper I was most interested in.

Q: More than the sports section?

David: Much more. And as a boy I used to watch all sports, even bowling! I remember the first stock I purchased; I bought one share of Swank. They made Jade East cologne for men.

Q: Yes, I remember Swank. They also made cheap costume jewelry that would break exactly three minutes after you got it out of the store!

David: What a memory! And I did my fundamental research too. Two colognes were vying for #1 back then: Jade East and Old Spice. I guessed wrong!

Q: What attracted you to trading?

David: As I look back—and I've thought about this many times over the last 30 years—I always had an investing perspective. I believed in what I called the "rabbit theory" of money—let it multiply itself! So instead of just spending my money, I chose to invest it. And my $50 or $100 would not go very far in real estate, so I chose the stock market to follow. And as I said, I got going at 11 years of age looking at stocks and trying to get familiar with companies with the very limited information available to someone that age.

I remember I went to Detroit for my bar mitzvah. I had stock in a company called Sunasco. One of my relatives who was a stockbroker asked about the stocks that I owned and when I mentioned this one he freaked! "Sell! Those guys are crooks and the SEC is investigating them!" Well, I ended up selling it a few months later and many points higher. I remember I made something like $1,000. Wow! What an incredible amount of money that was for me at the time. But that was the summer of 1968. Everything went up then.

My family started calling me the "king of crap" for the kinds of companies I was buying. I suppose it was only fitting that my next purchase was Commonwealth United. Remember that one? Its ticker was "CUC" but I learned later that everybody on the floor called it "kook!"

Q: When did you decide that you wanted to trade as your profession?

David: In November of 1989. I had just left Merrill Lynch, where I had been a retail broker, and I was wondering what I would be doing next. I was doing much better financially trading for myself than the net commissions I had been receiving. That's why I left Merrill but it didn't click till one day I was reading the Ed Seykota interview in Schawager's *Market Wizards* and bam! It all fell into place. This was the career for me! I've been doing it now for more than seven years.

Q: You liked the idea of being judged solely on your own performance?

David: Among other things. I also like the money.

Q: What was it about that that appealed to you?

David: You have to understand that to me it was just a cleaner form of compensation—fewer layers. When I made money I shared it with only two partners: my mistakes and taxes.

But I would be remiss if I didn't mention the intellectual challenge—understanding chart patterns, trendlines, and psychology. How did my personality fit the market? Did we "spoon"? I love it. Still do.

Q: Do you think you had a natural talent for trading or do you think it was more of a learned skill?

David: Both. To just say it was natural talent strikes me as arrogant. Looking back, I realized there was some talent but I've also invested more than 30 years boning up on my trading skills.

Q: How have you done that?

David: I must have read hundreds of books related to the field—at least it seems so! Trading, technical analysis, mental analysis including *very* basic accounting, attending seminars, networking, going through that great training program Merrill has for retail brokers. I've been lucky.

Q: How so?

David: In many respects everything I've ever done in my life helps me to now be a successful trader. At least *I* think so.

Q: Did you have a defining moment in your trading career?

David: In fact, two. One on the upside and one on the downside.

Q: Could you talk about those experiences?

David: It's funny. It's Hegel's thesis-antithesis-synthesis rubric. Up until the first trade I was always trading for fractions. The more money I had, the more shares I bought. But I always sold for my half-point profit. But in 1986 I bought a lot of Blockbuster Video. I held that stock for days, which became weeks and then months. I was familiar with the company, I understood what they did and so I was comfortable sitting through the oscillations. I picked a price I thought represented fair value and waited. And waited. And when I finally sold I was ecstatic! I remember Steve

Shobin, who was an analyst at Merrill Lynch then, asking, "How did you hang on all this time?" My answer was, "Who knows? But I did and I'm really happy!"

Q: That's a good answer.

David: From that moment forward, I was less a day trader and more a position trader.

Q: You said there were two trades. What was the other?

David: My antithesis. The first trade taught me to hang on. The second taught me humility and the power of stops. I had been holding a stock for about 1½ to 2 years and as I sat through the corrections and new bases I ultimately amassed about 50 points profit in the position.

Q: And what happened?

David: It went down. And down. I kept telling myself, "It's only a correction" but I was missing it. I was missing the big picture. Lower highs and lower lows, down 30 percent from the high, 40 percent, 50 percent, but I had vision . . . "Wall Street sure is stupid," I kept telling myself.

Q: What you describe is not a correction; that's a bear market!

David: Exactly. I learned the hard way the truth of the adage, "Bear markets teach you to trade, bull markets to hold." I finally sold 50 percent down. Ouch!

Q: What did you learn?

David: Stops. Use them. Know when to get out to protect profits as well as capital. So Lesson #1 would be: Patience until fulfillment. And Lesson #2 would be humility—I can be wrong, so be quick to act on what the market is telling me because *it* isn't lying to me.

Q: What do you think is your greatest strength as a trader?

David: Discipline. Even if I think a stock is going straight up, when I assess a top price I'll pay, then that's all I'll pay. Same for the downside; if it violates my stop, I'm gone.

Q: You experienced a tragic event in your life about a year ago. Could you talk about it?

David: Sure. It was March of 1995. I was having a great year trading. I enter every year with the goal of earning at least 100 percent and I was already up 100 percent in March.

Q: And you've been able to achieve this kind of performance every year since 1989?

David: Every year but 1992. But it's not difficult to achieve when you start each year with $1,000.

To answer your question though, I have to backtrack for a moment. When I was in high school I had this irrational fear that I would go blind. Of all the senses I could lose it was my sight I feared losing most. It was just this anxiety that I would lose my sight before I could read all the books or travel to all the places in the world I wanted to see.

So one day in March 1995 I was driving to Palm Springs with my fiancée, Claudine, and her parents, who were visiting from Belgium. I was driving along when things went slightly weird. My vision was crossing like I was cross-eyed, or so it seemed. I removed my distance glasses and drove on. Over the weekend, my eyesight worsened mildly. On the drive home, I had my head propped up at a sharp angle and I was focusing on the road with 100 percent concentration. Everything seemed kind of screwy. It all looked wrong and right at the same time.

Thank God we made it home. The next morning, Monday, I woke up, walked out to the front drive to pick up the newspapers and as I looked up my street to the main boulevard, I discovered that things were darker than they should have been. And crossed. I was getting twin, dim images. I struggled through the newspapers and the day. The next day was even worse, so bad that I raced off to UCLA to see an eye surgeon I know. The surgeon prescribed new glasses to compensate for what was happening. Two days later, the optician had the new glasses so I rushed off to pick them up, but they were worthless: they didn't help. The optician was amazed; he had never seen anything like that. My vision was now deteriorating so rapidly the doctors couldn't keep up.

I went first to an ophthalmologist, who referred me to a neurologist, who took the MRI scans and then referred me to a neuro-ophthalmologist, specialist within specialties, layer upon layer. My regular doctor put me through a number of additional tests including 20 or 30 different blood scans. Nothing. No answers. They called it ideopathic. I found out later that means the pathologist is an idiot, he doesn't know the cause.

I lost 90 percent of the vision in my left eye and about 60 percent in my right and none of the specialists knew what was going on. One doctor recommended immediate surgery but another said that might be folly, that because they didn't know what brought on the condition they didn't know if it might self-correct. And if it did and I had had surgery, then it might be back again to the operating room for me to reverse the initial surgery. And I'm asking the doctors, is it psychosomatic? Maybe I just did it to myself! If there's no medical explanation, maybe *I've* done something. This was, after all, my greatest fear.

I can't stress enough how confusing this was for me. I mean, what do I do now? Should I compensate for my lack of eyesight and adjust my trading accordingly? And how do I do that? Who do I ask for help? Or, should I just sit back and wait, not trade, and *hope* that my vision returns to normal or that the doctors could do something to normalize it? Talk about trading emotionally: On the one hand I had fear, on the other, there was hope!

Q: And amazingly, as suddenly as your sight disappeared in March, it reappeared in mid-May?

David: Yes, I was lucky.

Q: Now that you have regained your eyesight and still have never discovered a cause for the blindness, do you think it was your body's response to the emotional stress of trading?

David: You and I spoke about that in Las Vegas and I have thought about it and even queried my regular physician. I have a very holistic attitude toward my trading and my personal life. I'd like to think that there is some connection between the two, but I was told there was not.

Q: It still sounds as though you have your doubts.

David: Absolutely! This was the low point of my life. I realized my greatest fear in the world—I went blind. If the doctors couldn't come up with a physical explanation, then there must be a mental or emotional one. You're the person who really got me thinking this way.

Q: What conclusion did you reach?

David: That there was a connection. Please understand that, in my opinion, a successful trader's trading life bleeds into his personal life and vice versa. After my nasty drawdown year of 1992, when I had that second defining moment, I got away from what I most enjoyed about investing: finding growth stocks that had a product or service that fundamentally changed the way we lived. Now I traded patterns, pure and simple. It didn't matter what kind of company, so long as the pattern looked good. Ultimately, I started trading an extremely high-probability, very low-risk pattern—it was coiled and ready to explode.

Q: And?

David: I was just like my patterns: coiled and ready to explode. My life was spinning out of control, I had too tight a grip on things. I was becoming impatient, even an asshole. Even life's small annoyances were provoking extraordinarily large responses from me. I was even screaming at other drivers on the road.

Q: You're not the only one!

David: But I was out of control. I had such a tight grip on my trading and I thought, on my life. Boy, was I wrong. I no longer liked myself or my trading. I had to change.

Q: How does this relate, do you think, to your loss of vision?

David: Something had to give and fortunately it happened *to me,* not something I did to someone or something else. Now, I want to have much more balance in my life, but that means much more balance in my trading, which may mean I can't approach it with my usual clinical detachment. I must be willing to sit through more of the oscillations. Because, if you have emotion in your life it includes joy and fear, disgust, likes and loves, greed, even yearning. If you trade dispassionately, in a way it means you just don't care!

Q: You're kind of blind to everything that's going on around you!

David: Yes! You just have rules. And you know, life does not resemble a chart pattern, it is not the market in that hard-and-fast way. Life is not black and white. There is gray. You cannot have an argument with your spouse and say, "I stop you out!"

I guess what I'm saying is that you can't be blind to these feelings. To be an effective trader, you have to be a human being with *all* that includes. You just have to be open and available to everything, good and bad, that comes your way.

And so I say to myself, intellectually, if I want to have more emotion in my life, I must allow myself more emotion in my trading. And if I allow myself more emotion in my trading, well that's the swing in prices. I must allow for those swings and the probability of more frequent losses. I don't want that, but that's how I see things now.

You said something that has now become my mantra: "Think in probabilities but act with certainty."

Q: Would you say that traders are different than other people?

David: Yes and no. I don't mean to hedge. Yes, we're different in the sense that we're always trying to make connections, like John Murphy's Intermarket Analysis, between two seemingly unrelated facts or data.

Q: For example?

David: Well, when Mt. Pinatubo erupted, immediately traders started thinking about its impact on the commodities markets and placing their bets accordingly. I don't believe most people think that way. But now. . .

Q: What changed?

David: What I learned was that I have limitations. Before I had this experience I would have gone on and on about how different traders are from other people. Now, I think that's bullshit. We're just like everybody else.

Q: What was the experience?

David: It was June of 1995, the month after my eyesight returned, and I felt the need to challenge myself, to break out of my rut. I decided to go on an urban version of a "walkabout." Claudine dropped me off at the Santa Monica Mountains to fend for myself, just camping and hiking for a week. Claudine and I are veteran hikers, we must hike 50 miles a week, usually 15 miles at a time. For some reason, during this hike I found some ridges too difficult to climb. Maybe I was hungry, but I just couldn't climb them, and after a while I said to myself: Maybe I'm not as strong a person as I thought. And for the first time in my life I was able to live with that.

There's more to the story. Two weeks later, Claudine and I and another couple are hiking in the Grand Canyon, Havasupai to be exact. It's a beautiful place! Anyway, we're hiking along to this one waterfall and getting to the bottom required a very strenuous and very steep descent. It's straight down this very craggy, volcanic-like rock where there's no ladder and no steps, just cuts in the rock and a metal chain for about 100 feet. I must have gotten 80 to 90 percent of the way down when I reached a point where the mountain turned under itself so all I could see was air and then the ground some way down. I freaked; I froze. I couldn't go either way. My mind was telling me to do one thing and my body was telling me to do another. I just sat there for probably 15 minutes. I feared I couldn't climb back up that stretch, after all, I'd just learned that I was not as strong a person as I had believed, but I couldn't go down. I was afraid. I had a fear of heights! Finally, I said screw this, and I turned around and climbed back up. This was a seminal moment for me. I finally, really, learned that I had limitations. And that, as human beings, we're all the same.

Q: So what you learned from that experience is that you're human?

David: Yes. Exactly. We can say we're different, we can even dress differently or drive different cars, but in the end, we're all human. We're all subject to emotions including fear, greed, and hope. Bottle up your emotions and what do you have left?

I think the real question is how traders differ from each other. I strive to find and achieve some balance in my life. What I do for a living is not all I do. I love to read voraciously and travel, and the game of chasing the ever-growing bank balance no longer interests me. If my analysis shows correction or even bear market, I simply sell and go away. I no longer feel the need to make every trade.

As traders, we can always make money, but as people how and when do we enrich ourselves? That's all I want now: enough money to live well and to travel and read. All those things that make us happy.

I'm reminded of a quote from Hippocrates: "Life is short, the art long, opportunity fleeting, experience treacherous, judgment difficult."

CHAPTER 10

A View from the Bridge

Marshall Stein

Mr. Stein is senior vice president of Rand Financial Services and a member of the board of directors, Chicago Mercantile Exchange. He is an independent trader and former member of the Chicago Board of Trade.

Q: What first attracted you to trading?

Marshall: What first attracted me about the business was that there were so many things you could do. You could be a floor broker or you could be a customer's man or you could trade for yourself.

As an initial idea, I don't think I came to the exchange to be a trader. I was looking for a place where I could do a variety of challenging things to make a living and here was a place where you didn't have to be one thing only. You could get a deck and execute orders for individuals or institutions on the floor or you could have a client-centered business or you could trade your own account. So it allowed for a certain versatility that I was looking for.

Q: Do you think there was anything in your background that prepared you for a career in the trading?

Marshall: I've always been disciplined about things. If I set my mind in a certain direction, that's what I'm going to do, and frankly, the conditions that are around me seldom change my thinking. I have prepared for those conditions before I've made my ultimate decision.

Q: You've been around the exchange for a long time, 35 years. You're well known in the trading community and you've seen a lot. What was your first impression?

Marshall: Well, I have to say, that as small as the exchange was—and it was, 35 years ago—for a young man coming out of college, it was extremely impressive to walk onto the trading floor. I had never seen anything like it. It was incredibly exciting!

Q: What was it that you found so exciting?

Marshall: The whole atmosphere was exciting. You had people in throbbing circles shouting at each other, gesticulating like participants in an athletic event. The expressions on their faces: pain, delight, and everything in-between!

Q: Did you feel like you belonged?

Marshall: Well, yes, as I just said the atmosphere was very athletic. When I was younger I had been an athlete and it felt like I was going into the big game. I found it both exciting and interesting. And then, of course, let's not forget this game that everybody was playing was what they were doing for a living, and it paid very well. Hell, that was an interesting set of circumstances!

I remember also you could pick out the people who were substantial and the ones who had done well. I also remember how impressed I was when I saw all the leading firms: Merrill Lynch, Paine Webber, Bache and Co. There were international banks represented. There was just this overall feeling of "big," and "important" even at that time.

Q: And being part of something much larger than yourself?

Marshall: Right, and for a young man just coming out of school, it was an awesome feeling.

Q: Your career has been different from those of most traders. You've traded on the floor as a member and also owned three different clearing firms. Could you talk about your involvement in the futures business?

Marshall: When I came into the business, the first thing I did—and I think it was a natural thing to do—was to look at who were the most successful people in order to develop my own business plan. I decided almost immediately that to be at the top of this business you had to become a clearing member, what we call today an FCM (futures commission merchant), Within a year's time I had a partner and formed an associate brokerage firm, which meant we had our own company. We were an independent brokerage business but cleared our trades through a primary firm. The next step was to form our own clearing firm and that was accomplished a year later. The name of our firm was Kamen Stein & Associates.

Q: What was the retail business like 30 years ago?

Marshall: We got our customers from various sources, as we do today; however, our major source was the *Wall Street Journal.* A small ad in the *Wall Street Journal* would bring a tremendous number of leads. We would get on the phone and call these leads and try to develop business. In the early days we literally used to sell to people who would come to visit the exchange. My partner and I would go up to the balcony, sit down and talk with the people in order to find out if they needed a broker and, of course, we were available to handle their business! We would go to conventions, you name it: There were the American Meat Institute conventions and all sorts of agricultural meetings and conferences, anywhere to develop business.

We also had some very interesting situations. We had a broker who had just started working for us. He was very good on the phones and had gotten some customers and was trading their accounts. At the end of one unusually busy day in which he did a lot of trading for his clients, he started screaming uncontrollably and we couldn't figure it out. Everyone in the office was running around saying, "Oh, my God, oh my God, what happened?" And this guy didn't say anything, he was just clutching his head like he was having a stroke or something. Finally, he looked at me with this stare of death on his face and said "I reversed all of the trades that I made today. All the buys should have been sells and all the sells should have been buys."

Q: How'd he do that?

Marshall: He just wrote the orders on the wrong side of the trading ticket. So the next day he was scrambling to get out of trades, make adjustments, resolve out-trades, and so forth.

Q: How'd his customers end up doing?

Marshall: Actually, it worked out very well. It was amazing!

Q: So much for broker trading!

Marshall: There is a similar story where Ray Friedman who, as you know, started Refco Trading, was given an order in the old egg pit to sell 300 contracts and, instead of selling them, bought them in error. Immediately after he realized the error the market went up the limit. What should have been a terrible loss turned into a tremendous profit! The market went dramatically higher over the next three or four trading sessions. And the story goes that the money was used to buy his clearing firm, which today is one of the most successful firms in the industry.

Q: At one time you had branch offices around the country, didn't you?

Marshall: Yes, we did. We had ten branch offices. We had six branch offices in California alone, with our main office in Beverly Hills. The manager of the Beverly Hills office was also responsible for supervising the other offices in Santa Barbara, San Bernardino, Santa Anna, San Diego, and other California locations. We had a whole program that was set up in which we conducted seminars and workshops to develop brokerage business. After a while we started to notice a few things about the books that appeared irregular and we suspected foul play.

Q: What did you notice?

Marshall: Well, I don't remember exactly, but I knew there were irregularities. Trades being placed after the fact and things like that.

Q: You had ample reasons to suspect that something was wrong.

Marshall: Right, and when we found out for certain it was like on a Friday morning about 11:00. As I recall, our bookkeepers called us and said something strange was going on: unexplained transfers of positions and monies into accounts. I knew we had to do something about it and do it immediately. We wanted to catch the manager before he went away for the weekend, with his hand in the cookie jar, so to speak.

So I'm asking myself, my word, how can I leave the Chicago office, we've got the rest of the trading day and I've got a lot of things to do? My partner and I were very excited and were just trying to figure what to do.

So Richard says, "Look Marshall, I was going skiing this weekend, I have clean underwear and everything packed in my car, let me go out there and handle it." And I said, "All right. You go out there, notify the manager that we know what he is up to and that we plan to report him to the appropriate authorities." I should point out that my partner was a former police officer.

We had the secretaries calling to get an airplane reservation and because it was last-minute, could only find one flight that had availability; it left in an hour. So my partner, as a former police officer, picked up the telephone, called the Chicago Police Department. They had a car waiting for him at the expressway with a siren that delivered him straight to the airport and had a police escort waiting for him in L.A.

The manager didn't show up for work that day, so Richard went straight to his house in the valley. He knocked on the door a few times but nobody was at home. So he decided he was going to wait for him. He waited for three or four hours. At about 11:00 that night, the manager and his family came home. Richard jumped out of the bushes and literally captured the manager.

I wasn't there, so I don't know all the details, but knowing my partner, I don't think there was any resistance by the manager! My partner was basically a very excitable person. I could almost envision what was going on there. But what I didn't learn until later was the most interesting of all.

My partner kept saying, "Don't worry Marshall, I've secured the situation." What I didn't realize until later was that "securing the situation" meant that Richard had chained the manager to his brass bed for the whole time that he was out there. He gave the poor soul just enough slack so he could go to the bathroom, until we got whatever assurances that were necessary that all irregularities would be covered. While he was there with the manager chained to the bed, he had the manager's wife washing his underwear and ironing his clothes and giving him whatever else he needed! I swear it's the way it was told to me!

I had another manager that I had a difficulty with—I hope it's not beginning to sound like we always did. This guy was putting trades into a fictitious account. It was necessary to confront him. I had our attorney, who was in Beverly Hills, make an appointment with him. I flew in from Chicago just to fire him. When he saw me in the attorney's office, he was stunned; he had been talking to me just hours before in Chicago. He says, "What are you doing here?" I told him, "I think you know!" It was the end of his career in trading. He was a former concert violinist.

I had him sign notes and so forth, but I think I had to pay off some very substantial amounts because of his shenanigans!

Q: I guess 30 years ago there were a lot of flimflam men in the futures industry.

Marshall: One broker who was working for me was in debt to us up to his eyeballs. He wrote me a letter and told me that he just moved from his one-bedroom apartment to a nicer place. He said, he thought being able to entertain prospective clients would help secure a higher-quality business. I didn't think much of it at the time but a month later I was invited to a party at his house. Remember, now this guy didn't have a nickel to his name! I remember driving up to his house. It was in Sherman Oaks. As you approached the driveway, large metal gates opened, followed by a very long driveway up to a magnificent house. There were large grounds with a bandstand where musicians would perform.

Q: Like a gazebo?

Marshall: Well, it was more than that. There was a whole setup where musicians would play. Again, he didn't have any money, but he was leasing a Rolls-Royce that was parked in the driveway. It was all about the California lifestyle. You know, showing clients that they're going to a mansion or to some very substantial place.

Q: And of course, he represents to any prospective clients that he's from Beverly Hills or Sherman Oaks or wherever!

Marshall: Oh yes, he lives in Beverly Hills. That's the important thing. This particular guy used to have an expression. He used to say, "I'm on canned goods." Being on canned goods meant that he would buy a can of fruit cocktail, and in the morning for breakfast would eat a third of it, for lunch a third, and for dinner he'd finish it off. The guy was always "on canned goods."

Q: But you still make your payments on your Rolls.

Marshall: Well, you still have that Rolls going if you can keep it away from the repossession guy. This same person would go to a fancy restaurant and tip the maître d' $30 and the waiter $25. He'd be starving the rest of the month but he'd be living what he called "the lifestyle" and cruising Beverly Hills for fun and profit!

I remember once on a visit to my Beverly Hills office one of the other brokers took me to a drugstore on Wilshire Boulevard. He was showing me the things that he was really interested in. Here was a guy who had a negative net worth and he was showing me hairbrushes for $900 apiece. He said to me, "There: Do you see those incredible hairbrushes?" "Yes." I said. "Boy," he chirped. "I love those hairbrushes." Can you imagine? They're $900 a piece for a hairbrush and he'd be happy as a lark to own one. He was kind of shocking me a bit. He was willing to buy that brush and be "on canned goods" for the next three months. That was the mentality!

Q: Marshall, do you think the industry still has people like that in it?

Marshall: I do. I was in Florida recently on business and saw some brokers who I think have similar personalities; maybe not quite as drastic as they were years ago, but guys cut out of the same cloth.

Q: How do you think the retail side of the business has changed in the last 25 years?

Marshall: It has changed considerably. The industry as a whole is much more professional. We've had a downward spiral of commission rates, which has made clients more sophisticated and more aggressive about knowing with whom they are doing business. There is also institutional business that we didn't have in earlier times, so the volume and professionalism has increased considerably.

Q: Do you think the average retail client is a more sophisticated customer today?

Marshall: Absolutely. Twenty-five years ago very few people knew anything about commodities. I'm amazed today. I have clients who know as much after five or six months of trading as I did after five or six years!

When I came to the exchange in November of 1960, I think there were only one or two books written on commodities. Today there are hundreds, maybe thousands! Today's investor is a much more serious and knowledgeable trader.

Q: After 35 years, what is it that you like so much about the trading business?

Marshall: I love being around the traders. Traders are fun-loving, exciting, interesting people. I mean, at the exchange we have Ph.D.s and we have guys who barely got out of high school. But they're interesting and alive people who are very good at what they do and I enjoy being in their company. I think it gives me a feeling of vitality!

Q: Can you think of the best moment in your career?

Marshall: Being elected to the Chicago Mercantile Exchange's board of governors. It was very exciting to receive that kind of vote of confidence from my colleagues. It was a great thrill for me.

Q: Did winning the election feel as good as your first big trade?

Marshall: I would say better, much better! After all these years to have that level of trust placed in me by my fellow traders was extremely gratifying.

Q: Who stands out as the most memorable character you've met in your career?

Marshall: Sydney Maduff, with whom I owned Maduff, Kamen and Stein. When I first came to the exchange, Sydney was "the man." I mean, he was unquestionably the leading trader on the floor of the exchange. He was a very gentle and kind person. That aspect of his personality really stands out. He had probing eyes and a very keen mind.

I had only been on the trading floor for three weeks back in a time when floor traders hardly ever spoke to new members until they proved themselves and Sydney just out of the blue walks up to me and asks what I think about the market. It was a thrill for a guy who had been here just three weeks to have the leading trader on the floor, maybe even nationally, come over to him and ask what he thought of the market. Of course, I gave him an opinion, but I also added, "Mr. Maduff, I couldn't imagine that you'd be interested in what I could have to say."

Q: Did he follow it?

Marshall: I don't know, but what stands out is how respectful and serious he was. He made a kid like me feel that he was genuinely interested in what I had to say. I think maybe that was part of his success, that he was a willing listener. He could learn something from an unexpected source. Eventually, we became partners.

Q: I remember Sydney very well. He definitely was a trader with very strong convictions.

Marshall: Yes. He definitely had an opinion. He was willing to listen to other traders' opinions, but he had his own opinion, and he would follow through with it. And he had some huge swings up and down, but he was very true to his own code. He had unshakable confidence in his own analysis until the market proved him wrong.

Q: What has trading taught you about yourself?

Marshall: Trading has certainly taught me about my personal strengths and weaknesses. It has taught me how I react under situations of stress.

Trading has allowed me to have a measure of courage in what I do for a living. It has shown me that I have the capability to rise to an occasion to exhibit, if you will, grace under fire.

It's not like I go around pounding my chest, but it's a comforting thought to know that I have the courage to trade markets at times when it feels like I should run scared. I can exercise strength of character to either stick with it or get out.

Q: In that sense, courage is also the independence of mind to act out your own ideas and have the conviction to stay the course in the face of other people's opinions.

Marshall: It's the analysis sometimes, or the work that you've done. It's the culmination of your thinking that you've put into action.

Q: What do you think distinguishes you from everyone else?

Marshall: I think what distinguishes me from most is that I have really done just about everything that is possible in our profession and that I am still on the lookout for new challenges.

Q: In the trading arena.

Marshall: I've handled just about every type of business from individual clients, introducing brokers, and professional money managers, to trading for myself as a market maker on the floor of the exchange. I have been a member of both the Chicago Mercantile Exchange and Chicago Board of Trade and have served on the CME board.

It's been an exciting and wonderful ride. I plan to trade and be at the exchange at least until I'm 85. Where else can I find such an exciting profession with such talented and fascinating friends? I have immense respect for them and I hope they have respect for me. They know me because they've watched me trade. They've watched the things that I've done for over 30 years. And I've watched them. You get to learn an incredible amount about a person when you see him operate in the crucible of the trading floor. You get to see what he's made of. What makes him tick as a human being and as a trader. Courage, generosity, pettiness, fear, respect. After 35 years I've seen it all! But I haven't seen so much that I'm not up for a good surprise! Sometimes I feel as though I am viewing this unbelievable 35-year pageant from the top of a bridge. It's happening all around me, and I just can't wait for what's coming next.

CHAPTER 11

Trades to the Beat of Her Own Drummond

Robin Mesch

*Ms. Mesch is the chief fixed-income technical analyst
for Thomson Research, one of the largest providers of
proprietary financial information services in the world.
She is a recognized expert on Drummond geometry.
Robin authors* Trading Prophets—CBT Bonds, *a fixed-income
market newsletter providing trading strategies and
analysis on the 30-year Treasury bond.*

Q: What first attracted you to trading?

Robin: I was a religious studies major at Brown University with
a big question mark as to what I was going to do after I graduated.
I was presented with an offer to learn a technical method for analyzing the market in order to help someone trade.

Q: At the time did this seem like a strange thing for you to do?

Robin: No. Actually, I jumped right in and gave it 100 percent
because I really liked the people I was working for and felt it was
certainly going to challenge me.

Q: With what specifically were you initially presented?

Robin: I was presented with a book on Drummond geometry.
I was asked to read it and make some sense out of it. It started out
as a very small project. My inclination in those days was to take
small projects and make them big!

Q: Was the person you were working with an academic?

Robin: He was a trader, and not a successful one—a struggling
trader who had success at one point and was then kind of hit over
the head by the market.

Q: Why did he come to you? Do you think that he thought you possessed a natural gift for the markets or was it your mathematical ability?

Robin: I guess I was bright and had a lot of energy and free time. And when you combine all those things, what did he have to lose? If anything, he had a lot to gain.

Q: Once you started studying Drummond geometry, did you find it challenging?

Robin: I loved it! In learning the material, I got to know and developed a relationship with Charlie Drummond. At the time I was reading his book, there were maybe only 50 advancers.

Q: Advancers?

Robin: The advancers were a select group of traders. For a small sum, you could become one. Charlie gave you a number that entitled you to speak with him and learn the system. There are 100 of us. The group was closed off some time ago.

Q: What was your number?

Robin: The person I was working with was number 7. Remember, I never paid for the manual! After I learned the system, Charlie gave me an honorary number, which was kind of sweet, and my own set of books. I think I was 69. Really, I don't even know. I'd have to look it up.

Q: What was it about Charlie Drummond that you found so interesting?

Robin: Authenticity. You knew the style was authentic. And how do you know that? After you would talk about the market and the trade, it would unfold. Charlie was genuine and he really wanted you to learn. He became my trading mentor. I don't know if you've ever had a mentor, but you know when you're being mentored by an authentic person who's not holding back. So that was just a cool experience for me.

Q: Did you get a chance to meet him?

Robin: Yes. We would meet and always in secret. He's eccentric and not a very public person. The trader I was working for and I would meet at an appointed location in Toronto. We would bring our computer and go through the material.

Q: With Charlie Drummond?

Robin: Yes. I loved the analysis. Initially, I didn't do any trading. I wasn't allowed to go behind the wheel for five years. I was just putting in the orders, doing the analysis, and making trade recommendations.

Q: What do you like about trading today?

Robin: It's funny, because I was thinking about that, trying to decide why I like trading so much. I'm a real control freak! I think there is probably no better job for someone like me: analyzing and determining what's going to happen tomorrow is about the ultimate control you can impose on the world.

Q: It must be frustrating for you when the world doesn't conform to your analysis. I mean, it seems like you're engaged in a perpetual activity of sweeping away the ocean with a broom.

Robin: That's right. It's hard. I mean, it is really impossible.

Q: But as Camus says, you have to conceive Sisyphus as being content. Otherwise, he wouldn't continue to roll that stone up the hill.

Robin: Right. Well, you do have to be an optimist too, because the utter impossibility of control is just a fact of market life.

Q: But, paradoxically, it does gratify this part of you that likes to control things. Of course, as you state, ultimately you can never have control because the market is so vast and uncontrollable in many ways.

Robin: You know what? Maybe I'm only intellectually aware of it because I go at it everyday with enthusiasm and naïveté. So, on some level I must not quite know that yet. I still feel like I'm digging into the market. During these past three months I have come up with something that I find is new about the market. And that gives me a new understanding of what's going on.

Q: Can you share that with us?

Robin: It's Market Profile-related. As you know, I work with that form of analysis as well. I feel that even Drummond's work for me has started to be more present tense than future tense. A lot of the earlier work that I did was projecting into the future.

Q: More anticipatory.

Robin: Right. More than looking at the actual flow of the market right now. And so I think his work has gone toward that and certainly concentrates more on the here and now.

Q: Are you saying your trading has become more . . .

Robin: Present tense.

Q: More locked into what's happening as the market is unfolding, rather than trying to project its next movement?

Robin: Exactly. And it makes you give up a few things. It makes you give up price for structure and it makes you give up a lot of projections so you just stay current. And there are projections within the present tense. For me, it means I've become much more of an intermediate-term trader, where my trading is less oriented toward specific prices in favor of the overall structure or profile of the market.

Q: Overall, what is it about trading that you find so fascinating?

Robin: It's a very competitive sport and there are not a lot of winners. What it means to me is that a lot of people aren't doing the right thing. So many people are losers that you have to wonder.

Q: Well you obviously don't see that as a reason not to participate. If anything, it sounds like it motivates you to be on the right side.

Robin: It does. My market analysis is very accurate. For me, the biggest challenge is to bridge the gap between my analysis and execution. I find that to be the essential issue in my trading.

As I said before, I started off just doing analysis for a good number of years on many, many markets, and that analysis was crystal clear. I mean, I could tell you where the market was going today, tomorrow, next week, next quarter! I could tell you this is the low for the month, this is the high.

Q: It's always a lot easier calling it from the stands than being on the field isn't it?

Robin: Yes, that's a great way of putting it, because there are so many things that come up while you're on the field playing the game.

Q: Robin, what do you find keeps coming up for you? Earlier you had mentioned this need for control. Is that something you have to work on?

Robin: Yes, definitely. That's the part of me that gets burned in the market. So I have to watch it very carefully. There's a phase that you go through where you think you can't lose. And you convince yourself you know exactly what the market is going to do next. Then to compound problems, you think since you can't lose, you might as well pyramid as the market is going against you. That's how strong you feel about that. But you need those experiences of being wrong so you can learn to become a disciplined trader, which in the final analysis is ultimate control. You learn from your mistakes if you're committed to paying attention.

I was in this big platinum trade. It was a tip.

Q: Were you trading for an institution then?

Robin: No. We were trading for our own accounts.

Q: You had your own trading group?

Robin: Yeah. And we were really confident on this one. And you know, the lower it went, ironically it just instilled more confidence that it was going to come back and that it hadn't really tanked yet. I mean, it wasn't going our way but it wasn't falling apart.

Q: And of course, the lower it got the more attractive it was to buy it, right?

Robin: We were all just waiting for the "big move." One day we came in and—oh my God, I had never seen a longer line to the downside.

Q: A bar chart line?

Robin: Yeah, a chart line. I thought it probably was a bad tick (bad price), but there it was glaring at us. We were in complete denial. We actually ended up putting a bedsheet over the computer for the day.

Q: Did that help?

Robin: The pain was so great, there was no other way to deal with it. And we weren't out, we still didn't get out! The bedsheet was just step one. Finally, the pain just got so intense that we just had to exit. Of course, no one was even thinking risk to reward at that point.

Q: It seems it got to a point where you either got out of the position or you had to purchase a new bedsheet.

Robin: Blanket. So it couldn't come out at you at night! This is just one of the many experiences I've had along the way to becoming a disciplined trader.

Q: Do you think there was anything in your background that prepared you for trading?

Robin: My music. I'm a musician and seriously thought about a career in music before I went to college. I've heard that the idea of pattern recognition, which is what I use in my chart analysis, is related to the ability to read and interpret musical scores.

Q: What instrument did you play?

Robin: I'm a pianist.

Q: Do you feel your music influences your trading?

Robin: I think it does. Music creates a flow inside of you. Maybe it creates the internal atmosphere for some intuition, which I think plays an important role in trading.

Q: And you stated the idea that your ability to recognize patterns may derive from your ability to read music?

Robin: And also to hear the music. There are certain qualities in musical phrases and tones and connections inside the melodies.

Q: The interconnectedness between the tones and the melodies?

Robin: That's right and there's a lot of detective work that takes place. In the same way I feel like a detective when I'm examining a price chart. I'm looking for connections. I'm looking for clues. A lot of times, I talk to the chart. I have thousands of studies on my charts, pictures and color codes by which I can immediately see and feel what the chart is telling me.

Q: So you definitely feel your early musical training and your continued interest in music has prepared you for trading?

Robin: Yes, I think it has been an invaluable experience.

Q: Robin, do you think your trading is more karma or dogma?

Robin: I think that is a great question. My take on it is a little different. I think it's karma and dharma and frankly has nothing to do with dogma! Karma means that you are going to attract situations in your life that you'll really have no control over. And if you're going to be rich, you can basically buy the lottery ticket. If you don't do anything except play the lottery ticket, that's the way it's going to happen for you! You hear people say things like, wow, this guy was a plumber. Why him? You can do it in any way. You know, pick your spot for whatever event is going to unfold for you. It's going to unfold and that's how it's going to happen. Buy the beans and wait for them to go limit up!

Q: That sounds like a very liberal attitude for a control freak.

Robin: That's only half the story. Being lucky is no crime! The other part is you are duty bound, I think, to dharma, which is working diligently every day at something. I feel that whatever I'm not exactly in control of with karma, I'm very much in control of with my work ethic and discipline, dharma. And if I don't do it to my absolute best ability, then I think my karma is not going to unfold in the most fluid way for me. I was presented with a book and charts and an offer to learn a trading system many years ago. My life has basically been taking that bone and chewing on it. Each time I chew on it, something unfolds for me. So it's still unfolding. The discipline and diligence and intellectual rigor, that's my dharma.

Q: Do you find with your trading that the more control you give up, the more control you end up having? Have you had that experience?

Robin: Well, maybe in life. But in trading?

Q: I was thinking about what you had said earlier in purely analytical terms that as you gave up the control, focusing more on structure than price, your trading has become more present tense.

Robin: Right.

Q: It just occurred to me that the more control you give up trying to anticipate market direction and the more you begin to just look at what the market is doing, you're much more likely to have a more present-tense orientation. Is that what you meant? Was giving up the control of price orientation what allowed you to become more responsive to the market?

Robin: I think that is very true. This whole thing about giving up price frees you to see the overall structure of the market. Being trapped in that price mentality really negates in many cases the internal logic on which the trade is built on.

Q: What you're saying is you need to give up control in order to have a more dynamic view about the structure of the market.

Robin: Right.

Q: And not focus so concretely on a particular price tick—to focus more on what the market is trying to tell you. In your case, what is the particular sonata that the market is playing? Sonata, not partita!

Robin: Right. So you really have to give up the control. And that can be very difficult. The last time we talked, I was very risk management-oriented. I've worked with both Pete Stutemeyer and Charlie Drummond, neither of whom even trade with stops. That's how their risk management is. They think stops are horrible! It's been hard for me to do that. But I have become much more relaxed in not putting in a stop, and letting the market prove my position wrong.

Q: I imagine the reason that they don't use stops is that they feel it gets in the way of having a more unified view of the market.

Robin: Well, two things. One does it because he feels he'll always get taken out. And the other feels it just tends to get in the way. And I can see how that can happen. For instance, there's been a long period, months of horizontal movement in the market and the market begins to separate away from that horizontal area on one end or the other. If you had such a huge background and the market moved away from it, it's going to take a lot to prove wrong. Some gyration back and forth around a certain tick is not significant. It's going to take a real reentrance back into that consolidation area.

Q: Or breaking through to the down?

Robin: So you have to be more elastic about the perimeters within which you are willing to trade and that is why I say I have become much more oriented to trade structure. And structure gives you a lot more time to make your decisions.

Q: What do you think is your greatest strength as a trader?

Robin: My analysis, understanding the market, really knowing where the market is going based on its underlying structure.

Q: What do you think is your greatest weakness as a trader?

Robin: Not believing in what I see.

Q: Not being able to act upon it?

Robin: Yes. I'll see something and I will tell my partner, I'll tell my broker, I mean, I'll tell the world. And then, there's this moment of hesitation. Sometimes I have to force myself to put the trade on because a lot of times my satisfaction derives from being right.

Q: The analysis.

Robin: It's being right, not necessarily making the money.

Q: Do you feel you have to discipline yourself to overcome that natural bias?

Robin: Yes. Because I get so much satisfaction in being right, I have to discipline myself to do the trade. It's not exactly fear. Sometimes I can take or leave the trading. But never the analysis—I'm addicted to that!

Q: What was your worst moment in the market? Was it that experience with the platinum trade?

Robin: That was bad but I had one that was even worse! It was a Eurodollar spread. I was trading for a large institution. At the time, I knew nothing about spreads, really, and I knew less about the Eurodollars! If you asked me what they were at the time, I couldn't tell you! I just got this idea about a Euro spread. It was at this all-time, can't-go-any-lower level. You know how that goes!

Q: In my experience, when they can't go any lower, that's usually when they're definitely not going higher!

Robin: I had put all these orders in for a pyramid and I was trading a lot of contracts. I went away on vacation. That's a confidence level! And I would call in every day and the spread was getting worse. I was telling myself that I was trying to stay disciplined and was really going for the long haul. I just kept building a losing position.

Q: You know, going away was just another bed sheet!

Robin: Absolutely. A vacation can be the ultimate denial! In fact, when it started to go down I stopped calling in. It was just too hard to know. I decided I was going to wait until the week was over. When I got back, it was a real mess. I probably drew down half the account, which was just devastating! I spent the rest of the year just getting back to zero. It was very demoralizing.

Q: How did you overcome that experience?

Robin: I just started over. I was determined never to do that again!

Q: What did you learn from that experience?

Robin: That trade was probably the biggest learning experience of my life. In the whole experience of trading an institutional account, I moved from being a trader to being a professional. I realized what big money was in the market and what big losses felt like. I am convinced you really have to experience what a big loss is before you can become a professional trader. I didn't let it shatter my confidence.

Q: You took a hit and survived?

Robin: Yeah. I survived and I started over. I looked at all my technical analysis, fresh again. You know, there's nothing more appealing than starting from base one, going back to the drawing board, and having a new beginning.

Q: Robin, what do you think trading has taught you about yourself?

Robin: It's made me more solid, more grounded. I've learned to develop a tolerance for pain. My tolerance for pain is really incredible. I feel like I can leave after a hard day of trading, go outside and say, okay, world, let me have it! It's been a long haul and a lot of work—a lot of hours and concentration.

I think I possess a pretty good humor and mellowness about trading. I keep it fairly contained to the trading room. Not only do I have a good sense of humor, but I have a light touch. I really do believe in that karma/dharma thing. I mean, I totally believe that the experience of analyzing the market, coming into work, coming up with the trade, all of that is what I'm supposed to be doing because it's giving me a lot of pleasure and fulfillment. So I don't worry. I don't take the losses personally!

CHAPTER 12

Is There an Austrian Magician in the House?

Scott A. Foster

Mr. Foster is president and CEO of Dominion Capital Management, Inc., a trading firm that specializes in global financial derivatives with $50 million under management. Before forming DCM in 1994, Mr. Foster was senior trader for AO Management Corp. Mr. Foster holds a bachelor's degree from Grove City College, where he studied philosophy and religion. He is also a professional magician and has given presentations internationally on the relationship between trading and perception.

Q: What first attracted you to trading?

Scott: Initially, I was interested in trading because my father was an investor. He was the vice president of the college I was attending, a small private school in western Pennsylvania. And although my father was successful in the academic world, he did much better with his investments. So I guess I'm following in his footsteps. Grove City College was one of the few colleges in the country that taught economics from the Austrian perspective.

Q: From an Austrian perspective?

Scott: Right.

Q: You've got to tell me more about that!

Scott: Of course, it is a little different than what you get at most universities. It was a more philosophical approach. Free markets, very laissez-faire. Not at all quantitative. Basically, letting the market decide what is fair value.

Q: More of an Adam Smith–like approach!

Scott: Right. The big argument on campus was not between, let's say, Democrats or Republicans regarding economic theory, but rather between the libertarians, whether you were Randian or non-Randian (Ayn Rand) as to how you related to supply-side theory.

Q: Sounds like a hotbed of economic radicalism!

Scott: It was something of a closed environment.

Q: Did your father teach at Grove City College?

Scott: Yes, philosophy.

Q: Is that why you chose to attend?

Scott: Yeah. I wanted to follow in my father's footsteps and be part of the academic world.

Q: To teach philosophy?

Scott: Right. I actually entered college as a computer and pre-law major with more of an interest in computers than anything else. I would stay up all night calling computers all over the world. I was heavily involved in hacking circles and that kind of thing. After my first semester at school, I got myself into a little hot water.

Q: How is that?

Scott: I managed to break into my professor's computer account and download all the final exams. I locked up a lot of different faculty accounts, and started sending e-mail messages back and forth between various professors who thought that they were coming from other faculty members.

Q: Was this a prank?

Scott: Yeah, I was just kind of having fun, and developed a password-snatching program, which at the time I felt was one of my own original ideas.

Q: Scott, so having said all this, what would you say was your initial attraction to the market? Was it the intellectual challenge of exploiting supply-side opportunities or was it a wider theater for playing pranks?

Scott: I was very bearish going into the crash of '87 and, in the traditional line of thinking, loaded up on gold stocks. I ended up losing a lot of money. That bothered me because several of my friends who were bearish bought options and did very well! This was my first exposure to things like futures and options. I was really fascinated and I spent the next year approaching the market from what you might call an academic perspective. I bought every book that I could find and read everything that I could lay my hands on that would give me some insight into the behavior of markets.

I became frustrated every time I would buy a book. I was looking for some kind of general consensus and it was not to be found.

Q: No universal, scientific method that works every time!

Scott: Yes, every book seemed to contradict the one that I had just read.

Q: That in itself is valuable information, isn't it?

Scott: Exactly, and I understood the significance of that. I have always been really obsessed with problem solving and puzzles. I was a chess player and Rubik's Cube fanatic. Trading seemed like a great challenge! So one year to the day after the crash, I opened a trading account. Really, I didn't have much money. I had just graduated from school. I was recently married, and I was still planning to go to graduate school.

I convinced a bunch of my friends that I could make money in the futures market; most of them hadn't even heard of the futures market!

Q: How did you convince them?

Scott: To this day I don't know how I managed to do that.

Q: Was it a compelling philosophical argument?

Scott: Probably more the possibility of making a lot of money. I convinced them I could make them a fortune!

Q: Did you really believe you could?

Scott: Yes, I honestly did.

Q: On what basis did you believe that?

Scott: It just looked so easy. I mean, looking at it and saying I can have this free leverage. It just seemed like such an obvious way to make money.

Q: I guess I should ask you, as a student of philosophy, what your method was for gathering evidence.

Scott: That's a good point and it's something we should talk about because it wasn't until later that I began to see how my background was affecting my trading. I didn't see it initially. I probably didn't realize it for several years until things finally began to come together for me. My initial experience with trading was a lot of success followed by a lot of failure.

Q: Which is fairly classic, isn't it?

Scott: Exactly. And just to give you some perspective, this is what happened: I went to my friends who basically didn't have any money either. We all took cash against our credit cards and pooled together about $20,000, which is how I started trading. The first week I made ten grand. The second week I made another ten grand. The third week I made another ten grand and the fourth week I made fifteen grand. I think I had only two losing days. It didn't matter what I did or how I traded. I wrote options, I did spreads, I day-traded, I traded financials and nonfinancial markets. Then I got involved in the coffee market! I'm sure you're aware that there's a trading adage, "Don't trade anything you can drink for breakfast." You know, avoid coffee, cocoa, and orange juice.

Q: I've heard people say don't trade anything you can eat or anything that breeds (hogs, cattle, etc.)!

Scott: Anyway, I shorted the coffee market into a Brazilian dockworkers' strike. The day I put on the position, the market closed 25,000 against me. It happened so quickly! I was in a state of shock.

I was up $65,000 for the account. I never felt any pain all the way up until that point. The news stories started coming in that the government was declaring the Brazilian dockworkers' strike legal and that this thing could go on indefinitely. The financial news wires were projecting where the coffee market was going to open the following day. Not only was I going to lose the rest of my profits, but I was going to lose the entire account, have a deficit, and owe the brokerage house money.

You talk about a sleepless night! I had never experienced anything like it. It's something I'll never forget for my entire life, the feel of cold sweat, looking at the ceiling, staying up all night thinking.

Q: What were you thinking?

Scott: I didn't know what I was going to tell my friends. I didn't know where I was going to come up with the money to make good on this. Remember, I didn't have the money in the first place to speculate, much less come up with additional funds. It was just an incredibly traumatic experience for me.

Q: And what was the result?

Scott: Well, fortunately the market didn't open up quite as high as was predicted. I still lost everything except for $10,000 in the account. If you look at the coffee chart, in December 1988, that market went from about 160 all the way down to about 70 or 80. I mean, it just collapsed after that. I think the high tick was probably me getting out. So to answer your question, I approached my friends and said here's what happened. I thought they were going to kill me, but they said, "Hey, you ran it up once; you still have ten grand. You can do it again." I thought about it for a day or two, and then started trading again. In three or four weeks I tripled the account. From then on I was hooked!

Q: What'd you learn from that experience, Scott?

Scott: I thought at the time I had learned a tremendous amount, but it took two or three more near-death experiences until I finally cured myself of overleveraging. You see, I didn't have a good understanding of money management. There's a lot more to trading than having a market opinion and then backing it up with a large position. There was a copper trade and then a grain trade before I learned the importance of not allowing the leverage to control me.

It's an agonizing thing when you leverage yourself to an extent that you really shouldn't. You can't stop thinking about it. Minute after minute throughout the day, every tick in your favor rejuvenates the hope that the trade is working out and every tick against you is a sharpened dagger being twisted. I couldn't eat or sleep. I would think about it all night long. You're constantly second-guessing and questioning yourself as to whether or not the position is right. I couldn't go on trading like that. It was really painful going through all this but I believe in the final analysis it was the most instructive thing that could possibly have occurred. Being that close to death, paradoxically, gave my trading a new lease on life.

Q: You are currently managing about $50 million. What do you believe in your background has prepared you for trading?

Scott: I think obviously the game playing and the interest in puzzles has always been a fascination and challenge for me. I also liked things off the beaten track. For example, I didn't ride a bicycle; I rode a unicycle. I never played Little League baseball; I was very much into juggling. I tended to gravitate toward what other people would tell me I couldn't do and I always felt, I'll show you that I can do it!

Q: Was the challenge for you not so much the uniqueness of the activity, but rather showing people that no one could determine what was possible for you?

Scott: I think that's right. For me, trading combined all of my interests into one: game playing, puzzles, computers, and entrepreneurial endeavors.

Q: You're forgetting one.

Scott: What's that?

Q: Magic! You're a magician!

Scott: I started magic at a really young age, probably around five or six. From that time on, I developed a particular interest in sleight of hand. I'd spend two or three hours a night in front of the mirror practicing sleight of hand for years and years, all the way through the middle of high school.

Q: Scott, when the market starts going against you, do you ever feel like it's engaged in an elaborate sleight of hand directed against you?

Scott: Initially, I found myself on the other side of the table where I was the one who appeared to have been fooled. Learning about specific things, like how the market discounts news or why a market tends to peak at the most bullish point gave me a sense of greater control. As I began to learn from different events why I was so badly fooled, I began to see some of the correlations with what I do in magic. What became very evident to me is that in the marketplace, as in the magic I perform, it is not reality that matters. It is the perception of reality. It is how things are viewed, how things are seen.

Q: Which is precisely what magic is all about.

Scott: Exactly. When I do a magic effect that uses sleight of hand, what I'm attempting to do is to take advantage of the way people think. We tend to see things in patterns, which is to say we see things according to how we've been trained to see by our own different experiences throughout our lives. As a magician, you use these natural biases against the person to lose him in the illusion that you're creating.

Q: Do you think there is an analogy between the way magic exploits our natural psychological biases and the action of the market?

Scott: Say you're watching an illusion. By the time you realize that the girl is no longer in the cage or the lion has disappeared, it's very difficult for your mind to go backwards and try to recreate the event to see how that could have happened. Your perception has been directed in a different way. For me, the same thing ended up being true in the market. I realized that by the time you hit a point in the trade when the market was finally rolling over, it was a change of perception. It wasn't a change in the fundamental reality of that market. Look at the stock market crash, how different the actual fundamentals were a day or two before and afterward. There was, of course, a gargantuan change of perception. That realization was particularly instructive for me. I felt like I was back on familiar territory. I started to think of the market in friendlier terms instead of fighting the illusion. I tried to put myself back on the performing side of the table.

Q: How would you characterize your trading?

Scott: I guess this is where my philosophical training enters the picture. When I started in trading, I gravitated toward both discretionary trading and using some systems. I made a lot of money trading discretionary and I was just barely covering my losses with the system. I couldn't figure out why this was happening. What I realized was it is easy to find something that works in hindsight, but trying to create something that's going to work in the future is a completely different story. In reality, the whole process of trading is to come up with a system of rules that you live by, what you'd call in philosophical language, epistemology. It's a verification of knowledge. So the question is, how do you know you know? How do you know what you have has any relevance in the future? It's easy to create this stuff in the past, but trying to verify by what authority it will have bearing in the future and will continue to work is something else!

I began to apply different things to my trading models that I was developing and to the rules that I was living by as a discretionary trader. I looked for some way to verify them. I knew from studying classical logic that a universal affirmative will imply a particular affirmative, but the inverse relationship is not true. A particular will not imply a universal. And since I could never gather all the data points out there, and I could never gather all the information, how could there be any certainty? This realization ultimately led me in the direction of probability. It was the only way!

So in general I would say my trading evolved from discretionary ideas into a more objective rule system where I'm 99 percent utilizing a systematic approach. But it's not mathematical. I don't use calculus or algorithms or moving averages or anything like that.

Q: It sounds like it's a nonlinear approach to the market. Is that correct?

Scott: I guess it depends on who you talk to. There are so many different ways to describe it. I take the approach that, to trade the market successfully, you need some type of edge, some advantage that you believe you have over everyone else. There are two different edges that I have tried to exploit in my trading career. One is based on correlations. It's finding markets at an even tandem and you watch them moving in opposite directions, and then key off one by trading the other, say the bonds and the S&P. You're constantly jumping from thing to thing, trying to stay one step ahead of your competition by finding the next correlation or inefficiency in the marketplace.

The other approach that I'm looking to exploit in the marketplace has really nothing to do with a particular market but rather with identifying inefficiency in all freely traded markets, regardless of whether they're futures, options, or equities. As I became a little bit more objective and systematic in my approach, I gravitated toward this approach.

Some people are critical of this view. They say, "Well, don't tell me that S&P contracts trade like corn." And I'd say, "Well, yeah, they don't, but at the same time, we only have data on the S&Ps during a bull market." I noticed that if we close down 700, 800, 900 points in the S&Ps, that the next day there is a tremendously high probability that the market is going to take out the previous day's lows. It seemed like there was some bearishness that hung over for the next day, and if the market moved enough, then people had to readjust their portfolios to this new trading level. Instead of day-trading, I began to hold my shorts for a second day looking for the market to break through the lows.

I wondered to myself, is this just something particular to the S&P market, or is this something that has nothing to do with S&Ps, and has something to do with how people react to all market extremes. So I got the computers out, and I began to ask the computer, let's look at all the data out there. Let's look at corn, soybeans, the cash S&P. Let's look at any freely traded market out there and try to test that idea. We're going back in time to gain an understanding as to whether or not you're exploiting something that is fleeting or something that's really innate as to how people react to price data. That's how we develop our trading laws. We do it by coming up with trading ideas that make philosophical sense. We look at the probability and then test it across all the different data points in order to verify its validity.

Q: So basically you're still doing epistemology.

Scott: Right.

Q: Except now, you're not just studying it, you're actually doing it.

Scott: Now we get paid for it!

Q: Scott, what do you think is your greatest strength as a trader?

Scott: I work very well in an unstructured atmosphere. I think my philosophical training allows me to deal well with noise and static. I'm not a bean counter. I don't need everything to line up just perfectly before I feel comfortable. If it makes sense to me, that is, the underlying assumptions are valid, all of the noise doesn't bother me.

Q: What has been your best moment in the market?

Scott: The first four weeks of trading, when I took a $20,000 account to $65,000. It felt bigger than life itself. It was tremendous!

Q: Actually, you were very lucky to have that experience so early in your trading career, to experience that feeling of euphoria and possibly even learn how to deal with it.

Scott: I believe that experience ultimately was the most important lesson I could have had. If I hadn't crashed to the ground shortly after that, I don't think I would have been able to continue as a trader.

There have been a handful of other trades that were particularly gratifying. Most of the trading I do now is very short term in orientation, two to three days in the marketplace. It's a highly statistical type of approach. We have an edge and we grind it out. I used to do a lot more of what I call campaign trading, where I had a fundamental idea about the market and I would trade around it. I used to do this type of trading a lot in the cattle market. Believe it or not, it was one of my favorite markets. I was able to catch several big moves in the spreads which I would plan out six, seven, eight months in advance. I just kept telling myself that these spreads were going to be dynamite when we got to a certain point in the breeding cycle. I would look for the cattle coming on feed with possible weather problems and so forth and was able to take an idea and follow my own systematic approach all the way through.

Q: Do you still trade the cattle market?

Scott: I haven't for about a year, but the traditional commodity markets hold a real soft spot in my heart, particularly the livestock and the grains.

Q: Well, there's a certain romance about those markets. You can employ a Hegelian view to identify the unconscious forces developing behind the market: thesis, antithesis, synthesis. On a philosophical level it's very appealing.

Scott: Cattle was one of the few markets that I felt very strongly that I had a grip on what was going on. I really felt like I had 90 percent of the pieces in the cattle puzzle, and that I could make a substantial bet based on that. Most of the rest of my trading has been geared toward trying to understand what I don't know and focusing on that aspect; what I don't know about a market and what could happen to hurt me rather than looking at it more positively. I realized I couldn't get all the puzzle pieces to the other markets, which is why I have gone in the direction of probabilities.

Q: Scott, is it fair to say that your edge is that you have this very disciplined, philosophical approach to the market, which allows you really to understand the probabilities of any particular trade that you're engaged in?

Scott: It has been obvious to me from the beginning that I'm dealing with the best and the brightest in the world. I believe that the smartest people in the world are not curing cancer; they are in the financial markets, because that's where the money is. And that if I am going to make a dollar, I have to pry a dollar out of somebody else's hands. And when you begin to look at it that way, that's when you understand that there are two sides to the marketplace. If you want to buy a contract, somebody's got to sell to you, and if he's going to sell it to you, he equally and oppositely believes what you believe or he wouldn't be doing it! When you begin to look at the marketplace in that light, you need to be certain about what is your edge. You have to do what makes you think you can compete effectively with these traders and institutions, trading firms that have a whole host of Ph.D.s and professional traders that have been there for years, with unlimited financial resources and research capabilities.

I was never under the illusion that I could outreach some of these firms when it came to understanding some of the fundamentals. For me, it was more a matter of concentrating on market tone, market psychology, and the more temporal aspects of trading.

Q: Dancing between the raindrops?

Scott: That's a good way to put it. The key is that you must know what your edge is and respect the competition because it is fierce: talented, hard working, and well capitalized!

Q: Scott, what do you think trading has taught you about yourself?

Scott: Oh, boy. It teaches you to expect the unexpected and be prepared for it! You end up in situations that you don't think you're ever going to end up in, where you're forced to make decisions. You can't delay. You don't have time to think about it. The market's trading, and you've got to get out of a position or you have to do something. You also find yourself in situations that you don't want to be in despite all the preparation. So you must be quick-thinking and nimble. You have to learn to understand and manage the leverage. You've always got just enough leverage to hang yourself, and nobody's there to stop you! What I have learned is that through trial and error and several near-death experiences, I have survived and am very good at what I do.

I know also that I've been able to come back from 70, 80 percent drawdowns, and then have gone on to make new equity highs. I have never not made a new equity high. And I've gone from day trading to spread trading to doing a variety of different strategies and styles in many different marketplaces. I think I'm very good at exploiting psychology. I really feel that I could go to any market that trades in the world and make money. You must know your edge at all times! I've talked to traders who have hit a losing streak and they can't figure out why they're not making money. I always ask them, "What were you doing when you were winning?" and sometimes they don't know what they were doing or why they were winning. They aren't able to identify what they bring to the market that is unique and allows them to exploit opportunity.

Q: What does Scott Foster bring to the market that's unique?

Scott: I feel it's more my psychological approach to the marketplace rather than any particular methodology. I gravitate toward identifying what works. I've gone for periods where I only traded the cattle market. I've gone for stretches where I've done nothing but trade spreads. I've gone for months where I only day-traded the S&Ps. Fortunately, all of those experiences have been positive. You must be flexible and versatile. You can't bet on knowledge of just one market or one technical or tactical approach. If you do, you find that suddenly the market changes and you are like a deer caught in the headlights.

Q: You're lost.

Scott: You're lost and paralyzed in the glare of a changing market. You need the ability to adapt. I believe that is my strength as a trader.

Q: Where do you think that ability comes from?

Scott: I'm sure it's a combination of my educational background and life experiences plus the way that I was raised. I come from a very achievement-oriented family. Also, I would never minimize the importance of my philosophical training. I've always had a strong belief that ideas are supreme. My mother used to argue with me. She would say, "A man with an idea is at the mercy of a man with an experience," and I would not accept that because I never thought that people's experiences were that reliable. I truly believed, in a philosophical sense, that ideas reign supreme. In the end, the ideal would win out over the experience. And that's probably the way that I approach the markets.

Q: Do you think the market is at your mercy?

Scott: No, because the market makes sense. I don't see it antagonistically. I mean, if I'm having a very difficult day I don't feel like it's out to get me.

Q: Not even once?

Scott: I guess there have been a few times when I bought the high tick, but really I go with the flow. I don't feel like losing days are bad days. It doesn't seem to have an adverse effect. I really look at the market as a kind of a curiosity. It's more of an intellectual exercise about the next thousand trades that I do. Will they end up hitting the statistical distribution of my past trading?

Q: Is it the same fascination of seeing your first rabbit pulled out of a hat?

Scott: I thoroughly enjoy magic, still do to this day. I love seeing a good magician boggle my mind, entertain me, and see how he fools the audience. I'm doing exactly what I should be doing. I just can't imagine not trading! When I was very little and practiced my magic, I used to have my mother take a card all the time. She used to ask, "Scott do you think I was placed on this planet to do nothing but pick your cards?" and I said, "Yeah!" I really thought the only reason she was there was so I could entertain her. And to a certain extent, I have the same view about the market. The only reason there is a market is because I need to provide for my family. It's an environment I feel so comfortable in that I feel it is custom-made. If I were in a position to change the way markets are traded to make them easier, or to have them trend more, I wouldn't! I'd leave them exactly the way they are—fascinating to look at!

CHAPTER 13

Learn to Learn

A. Thomas Shanks

Mr. Shanks is president and CEO of Hawksbill Capital Management, a Commodity Trading Advisor. He is a former "Turtle." The Turtles were a group of handpicked traders who were mentored by Richard Dennis.

Q: What first attracted you to trading?

Tom: Boy, that could be a long story. I was involved in blackjack for a few years. I was playing professionally as part of a team that designed, manufactured, and programmed a computer to be used clandestinely inside the casinos, but that's a whole 'nother story.

Q: Tell me. It sounds pretty interesting.

Tom: I used to play backgammon regularly and met a player named Frank Schipani, who had managed a successful professional blackjack team and about whom a book had been written called *The Big Player*. It was written by a fellow named Ken Uston who was a former vice president of the Pacific Stock Exchange. He became enthralled with blackjack and left the stock exchange to play blackjack professionally. I was interested in learning about blackjack and had a group of friends who were interested as well, so we talked Frank into teaching a card-counting class. We met on a weekly basis in his penthouse for several weeks to practice our

129

game. Meanwhile, Ken had met a guy named Keith Taft, who had developed a blackjack computer. Together they had refined it somewhat and bankrolled a team to use it. They were successful for a short time before they were "pulled up," that is, discovered, while playing in South Lake Tahoe. They had been using hand input at the time and decided that, in order to reduce the risk of being pulled up again, they would put the entire operation into shoes. They approached Frank about managing a team using this new approach and Frank just happened to have the makings of a team meeting at his house on a regular basis. This was all *legal*, by the way.

Q: What did they put in your shoes?

Tom: We put switches and batteries and a relay recessed into the arch of the shoe that buzzed against the bottom of your foot so you could feel the response that the computer was giving you as you input the cards. I spent three years doing this with Keith and his son Marty—my contribution was programming—and a handful of guys that we taught to use it. It was very interesting but not terribly lucrative. We made enough to keep body and soul together, but we didn't get rich by any means. Eventually I realized that blackjack was not a good career choice. When I left, I had very little money and no recent work history—you can imagine the résumé—and I was kind of stuck for what to do with the rest of my life.

Q: How old were you?

Tom: I was 31. One day I was driving down the freeway and noticed that the car in front of me bore a license plate that read "LRN 2 LRN." That intrigued me. He happened to take the same exit I did and turned in the same direction I was going. When we came to a stop sign, I pulled up beside him and motioned to him to roll down his window. I asked him if that was simply a philosophical admonition or if there was something more to it. He replied that he taught a class, so I asked him to pull over and tell me more about it. I'd always been interested in the psychology of learning, so I ended up taking the course. It covered a great number of aspects of thinking and learning including creativity and problem solving, and stress management. The final exam was to take all the techniques you'd learned and apply them to a problem in your own life. My biggest problem was pretty obvious: I had neither a career nor any prospects. Among other things, I took a battery of career-assessment tests. The upshot of the process was that it became clear that I would enjoy something in math and finance.

At about this time, Blair Hull, a friend whom I had met through blackjack—who had, in fact, been part of the team that was the subject of the book, and who is now a very successful options trader and the principal of Hull Trading Company—heard I was out of blackjack and offered me a job developing commodity trading systems. I didn't know anything about commodities, but this seemed to be a step in the right direction and an opportunity to learn a great deal.

We developed a system at his direction, which he used for about six months, I think. I remember the first trade well: This was the summer of 1983 and beans were already pretty high. I don't remember exactly where they were, but as I recall our first signal was to buy beans and we were filled at limit up. Within a few minutes they were limit down! That was my initiation to commodity trading. Trial by fire!

Q: That kind of experience does teach you something, doesn't it?

Tom: I'm not sure what . . .

Q: Humility?

Tom: Yes, and it warns you that there is danger out there.

Q: This fire does burn!

Tom: Certainly that. Unfortunately, I've had occasion to revisit that lesson. Anyway, the following year I was on a trip to Chicago on business, and on a complete fluke I ran into a friend who told me that Richard was hiring "trading trainees." I didn't know who Richard was, but found out pretty quickly. So I pursued that and was fortunate enough to be hired into the program.

Q: This is with Richard Dennis?

Tom: Correct.

Q: Were you one of the original Turtles?

Tom: I was in the second group. I began trading in January of 1985. It was an incredible opportunity to learn from one of the best minds, one of the most creative minds in the financial world.

Actually, two of the best minds: Rich and his partner Bill Eck-hardt. I couldn't say enough good things about these guys. I owe everything I have achieved in this business to them. I want to add that being a Turtle was also a lot of fun!

So, to answer your original question, the initial attractions that trading held for me were the excitement and the kind of money that was involved. It also seemed like it would be a kick to compete in that arena.

Q: Does trading still hold that same attraction for you today, or has it changed a little bit?

Tom: It's probably not quite as exciting, but that's fine. I like it a little mellower. But it certainly still has the attraction of being a tremendous challenge. If anything, that has only increased over the years.

Q: Do you think there's anything else in your background that prepared you for trading?

Tom: Well, I think, like most traders I had a relatively strong interest in games of strategy and games of chance.

Q: Did you have a favorite game as a kid?

Tom: Oh, I'm not sure that I did. I enjoyed cards and board games, and I liked playing chess.

Q: When I spoke to Mike Dever, he told me his favorite game as a kid was Risk. I thought that was very interesting. Mike said he liked the idea of being able to dominate the world.

Tom: I played Risk, too, and I enjoyed it, although I'm not sure it was exactly for the same reason—maybe it was.

Q: Do you think for you trading is more of a learned skill or natural talent?

Tom: More of a learned skill, in my case, than a natural talent. I think there are those that have a natural talent for it, but I believe that it can be learned and I think that Richard and Bill demonstrated that reasonably well in the Turtle program.

Q: What was it like being in the Turtle program, being part of a group of obviously very talented individuals?

Tom: It was a rare privilege. I think the selection process was designed to find people who had biases and talents that would lend themselves well to learning the skills involved in trading, but whether or not they had any natural talent for trading, I still don't know the answer to that.

Q: They were people who were able to LRN 2 LRN, right?

Tom: Yes, and they had certain perspectives on risk—risk assessment, risk management, and risk and reward—all things that translated well to the principles involved in trading.

Q: In general, I would imagine they were people who had a natural ability or inclination for game playing and calculating risk. Right?

Tom: I think that's true. It's one of the threads that runs through the group. Most of us had a strong interest in gaming and/or at least some facility with arithmetic.

Q: If you think about the collective performance of the Turtles over time, it is pretty amazing what they've been able to achieve.

Tom: It is. I think most of that is Richard and Bill's legacy. In truth, I believe it's more a reflection of the principles that they taught us than of our own ability.

Q: What was it about working with Richard Dennis and Bill Eckhardt that made the experience unique?

Tom: I think it's fair to say that these two guys are brilliant. To the best of my knowledge, their breakthroughs were made together. They worked on the research as a team, throwing ideas back and forth. They had a wonderful intellectual relationship in that regard. They are both very clear and original thinkers, especially when it comes to trading and understanding traders and markets. Some of the principles they taught were in the literature, but many they arrived at independently, and they were able to embody all of them in trading systems arrived at by studying charts by hand before the advent of computers. They also had a high regard and a deep respect for the role that personal psychology plays in successful trading. Fully half of the training we received from them was devoted to that subject.

Q: What was it about their thinking that you found so impressive? Was it the quickness of it? The depth of their combined intellects? Was it the fact they could put together disparate ideas?

Tom: All of the above, and piercingly perceptive creativity. They seemed to arrive at some very basic, well-grounded principles before most of the industry did, very fundamental kinds of things. The idea of cutting your losses short and letting your profits run sounds like such a cliché now, but they understood early how to do it systematically with consistency.

Q: Can you give me an illustration of the way Richard would approach the market?

Tom: As I remember, one of the things that Richard learned on the trading floor was that most floor traders didn't, at that time, want to assume the risk of holding a position overnight, and he thought that there was an insurance premium to be had in that. Richard saw that taking the other side of that risk presented a substantial opportunity for profit. He was one of the few traders on the floor, I think, who was willing to take a position home.

Q: Tom, did you have a defining moment in your own trading career?

Tom: Yes. It was 1985. I was short the yen going into a weekend G7 meeting, and the meeting had the effect of weakening the dollar substantially. The consensus that came out of the meeting was that the dollar was too strong. The currencies opened significantly higher on the following Monday and handed me a big loss. I was psychologically shaken by the magnitude of the loss and concerned that I had done something wrong. I immediately reversed the position because that was what the system said to do. I discussed it with Richard later and he assured me that there was nothing wrong with being short given the chart formation. (We were taught to ignore fundamentals like G7 meetings.) So I remember the pain of having such a move go against me and my electing to follow the system and reverse. One of Richard's favorite maxims was, "Do the hard thing!" Well, that certainly was hard to do, but it was rewarded very well: the currencies continued to move for many weeks in my direction. That was a reinforcing experience: Follow the principles, stick with the systems and you will be rewarded.

Q: What do you think is your greatest strength as a trader? Is it your ability to follow the system?

Tom: Well, given the amount of discretion I have used, I'm not sure that would be at the top of my list! Richard encouraged us to use what he called "flair" in our trading, but my experience over the last two years suggests that I should do less of that and rely more on the systems that I've researched. My greatest strength is having been trained by Rich and Bill, but my second greatest would have to be that I'm personally involved in research. In fact, I do basically all the research myself. I've been doing it since I started working with Richard as a way to validate what he and Bill taught. For my money, there's no substitute for it: It affords invaluable insight and perspective.

Q: What do you think is the most difficult part of trading?

Tom: Going through drawdowns and the uncertainty associated with that. You know, the uncertainty associated with degradation of systems over time; the uncertainty of not knowing whether the game has changed; having the patience to wait for the opportunities.

Q: Your cumulative performance over time is really quite astounding although you're currently going through a drawdown. Could you talk a little bit about that, what you're personally experiencing, and how you deal with it?

Tom: I think that anybody that goes through a drawdown questions whether what he's doing is correct and whether the systems are still viable, so there's a real struggle with that. For me, experiencing a drawdown is great motivation to do more research— "Pain concentrates the mind wonderfully" and all that. Research can be reassuring: When you go back through the data, you realize that drawdowns happen, but they don't last forever.

So you tell yourself that ultimately you will come out of it. It's obviously very hard on the client and your own state of mind, but it's part of the game. Meanwhile, you've got to take care of yourself on a personal level, make sure you're getting enough rest and exercise, and that sort of thing. Make sure you're bringing all your energy to the effort. So, besides research, there's a lot of personal management involved as well.

Q: What effect do you think your trading career has had on your personal relationships?

Tom: It probably hasn't helped them. It's a very time-consuming effort. And if you're trading the foreign markets as well as the domestic, it's not a nine-to-five job by any means. Trading really comes first for me at this point in my life.

Q: What has been the best moment in your trading career?

Tom: I think the most fun was being involved in the coffee market in 1994. I was lucky enough to get a complete position early, and at one point in that trade in late June and early July of 1994, coffee was on a spectacular tear—a once-in-a-decade move. We had some days where we had $160 million under management and I think we had some days where we made $20 million.

Q: That's a good cup of coffee!

Tom: Good days! When the coffee trade was rolling, it was pretty dramatic, just spectacular.

Q: What was the worst moment?

Tom: Okay, I can think of a couple of good candidates. Let's see—1991, the day that the war with Iraq broke out, I took a very large hit.

Q: In which market?

Tom: Gold, yen, and the petroleums.

Q: Oh, you got the triple whammy.

Tom: Yes, I did. I think we lost 25 percent in one day. That was a real shocker. I think I lost $10 a contract in crude oil.

Q: That's like getting stabbed in the heart. How did you recover from that experience?

Tom: I've survived a couple of those! I had another one in January of 1995 that I'm still struggling with. January's not my favorite month!

Q: But how do you deal with it? Do you go back and do retesting? Is that your way of getting through that kind of experience?

Tom: That's the thing that works best for me. Otherwise, I can get eaten up by it psychologically. I just enjoy working through it and going back and trying to find ways to improve things, examining what I did that I could do better.

Q: I believe that's the quality that really comes through loud and clear about you! You're willing to constantly refine and retest in order to find a better way. I think that's what separates you and other top traders from everybody else. The constant and continuous commitment to improve. Most traders are just willing to say hey, I did my best, and it didn't work! And they end up doing the same things over again.

Q: What has trading taught you about yourself?

Tom: You can't kid yourself in trading. You have to deal with who you really are, and take responsibility for all your shortcomings, which the markets have a way of revealing rather starkly. You have to confront all your fears and tame them. You have to check your ego at the door. The whole process can be very revealing.

I took an interesting psychological test many years ago. It separated people into two categories: Those who sacrificed accuracy for speed, and those who sacrificed speed for accuracy. I was in the former group: the "impulsives."

Q: Did that surprise you?

Tom: It was not a great surprise, but it was still a very valuable insight.

Q: How do you address that inclination in your trading? Is it something that you keep in mind, that you possess a natural bias toward being impulsive?

Tom: Yes. I have to; it can be a very dangerous proclivity. It can serve you well if it's applied in the context where you need to be nimble and respond quickly to something you perceive in the market, but more often than not, because the market can be so deceptive, it can lead you into doing things that aren't sound. It's easy to rationalize that you need to react *now*—but if you give in to it, it's probably going to cost you money.

Q: So how do you do it, since there is a large discretionary component to your trading?

Tom: I do a couple of things. One is to try to act in accordance with sound principles, another is to remind myself that when I deviate from the systems, I run a degree of risk for which I need some pretty good reasons. And then I have to try to honestly separate the reasons from the rationalizations!

Q: If you could start your career all over again, would you trade?

Tom: Yes.

Q: The rewards are worth the pain?

Tom: I think so. You learn from each experience. There's nothing in life that you can do that can guarantee that you're not going to go through some pain. Trading is certainly not a singular pursuit in that regard.

Q: Although when you're experiencing it, it seems like a unique variety, doesn't it?

Tom: It really does. And as you know, psychologically, trading is as difficult a career as I can imagine. That's also the challenge and the fun of it. It's something that I still enjoy very much. It's still fun.

Q: What about it do you find fun, given what we've discussed? Is it that you're a masochist by nature?

Tom: You might think so! But no: This is one endeavor that would weed out masochists very quickly! It's just a great challenge and a lot of fun to try to solve the puzzles you find in the markets—and the puzzles you find in yourself—and profit in the face of very stiff competition. There are huge institutions throwing hundreds of millions of dollars at this game all the time in an effort to figure out how to trade better. There's no shortage of competition!

Q: What do you think distinguishes you from everyone else?

Tom: That's a tough one. The most obvious thing is the degree of leverage I employ. It's one I may have to rethink! As you know, we're currently going through a long drawdown, and a larger drawdown than I ever expected to have to sit through. I hope to never have to go through this again. But having been here before, I know we can come out of it; we're not conceding defeat, by any stretch. We'll come out of it, and we'll come out of it better for the experience and for what we learn from it.

Q: What did you learn from the last time you had an extended drawdown?

Tom: That patience and diligence are rewarded. That profits will eventually accrue if you do the right thing and stick with it. That's the most important thing!

CHAPTER 14

Lady Luck

Arlene Busch

*Ms. Busch heads one of the world's most successful
proprietary trading groups for Refco, Inc. Previously,
she served as director of trading and risk worldwide for
Cresvale International Management. She traded as a local
for nine years at the Chicago Board Options Exchange.*

Q: Arlene, what first attracted you to trading?

Arlene: I've always been a games player. As a child I used to
play marbles with the boys, never dolls with the girls. I've always
been very competitive. I played racquetball and I'm a bridge master. And trading is the ultimate game!

I love the competitiveness of trading. I'm a type-A personality
and I have no patience, no patience whatsoever. Trading is instant
gratification and I like that about it!

Q: When did you start trading?

Arlene: I started in 1978 on the Chicago Board Options
Exchange.

Q: What was it like when you started?

Arlene: You used to go down on the trading floor and there
were no theoretical pricing models. There were no pricing sheets
provided by the exchange. We used to stand on the floor and the
markets were really wide. And as long as I would bid along with
everybody else and offer with everybody else, I made money. I

was relatively bright and relatively fast as a market maker, so I learned as I went along. And I just knew I could compete and do well.

Q: Was there something specific that you were looking at in the markets that you think was different?

Arlene: I think what I did differently was show up and be a woman! There were very few women in the industry and certainly on the trading floor in 1978. I was treated a little differently and that was to my advantage.

Q: In what way were you treated differently?

Arlene: The guys would always include me in the trade. The brokers would be nicer to me. My voice was at a different pitch, so when I bid or offered, the broker would instinctively hear me and hit me on the trade.

Q: So you think that worked to your advantage?

Arlene: Absolutely.

Q: I should tell you that I've interviewed other women who felt it was a disadvantage to trade on the floor. As a group they have felt it took them a long time to be accepted.

Arlene: Oh, no, that's not my experience at all!

Q: What attracts you currently to trading? Is it the same things that attracted you initially? Competition and the instant gratification?

Arlene: Those are two of the characteristics of this business that I still find stimulating; however, I don't trade anymore. I haven't traded since 1992. Today, as the head of a proprietary trading group, I like being able to help the traders, I like being able to support them. It gives me a tremendous sense of satisfaction to see them do well.

Q: Can you talk a little bit about how you moved from trading for your own accounts to developing a team of proprietary traders?

Arlene: I started trading in 1978. In 1982 I went to the Chicago Board of Trade and began trading a new product called bond options. I traded there until 1987. At the end of 1986, the options market changed. What was formerly a very wide spread market changed drastically. Trading houses like CRT and O'Conner came in. They had cheaper financing. Their game was to get rid of all the locals and turn trades for half a tick. When I started at the board you could risk $100,000 to make a million. When I left you were risking $1 million to make $100,000! I woke up one morning and asked myself what am I doing this for? And eventually I left trading for awhile.

However, what I learned was that too much of who I am is tied up with what I do. And I didn't like not working. So I went to my clearing firm, First Option, and said that I wanted to get back in the industry. They suggested that I set up a brokerage operation at the Liffe Exchange. I moved to England, loved London but hated doing brokerage. I found that if I was right, the client made all the money and if I was wrong, the client blamed me! I didn't like it and figured, if that was going to be the case, I should trade. So I went to First Option and asked them if I could trade for the firm. They flatly said no, indicating they didn't want traders.

I left First Options and joined a British firm, James Capel, where I headed up their Matif and Liffe operations. I set up the theoretical pricing models, I hired the traders, I ran all the desks. Concurrently, I also ran an OTC operation where I supervised their upstairs traders who did very well. However, it was a large bank, and I didn't think it was compensating me properly so I left. I joined another British firm, Cresvale, and moved to Tokyo. I was responsible for futures and options trading and hedging up the company's investment portfolio. Cresvale had raised $500 million for a fund that was involved in warrants and they needed to hedge up the risk. It all worked really well. However, at the end of 1991 and the beginning of 1992, the Japanese market started to dry up, and so did the trading. I moved back to London and set up a futures and options group for Cresvale. We had three additional areas of business: equities, convertible bonds, and warrants. The head of these areas lost a significant amount of money and I was asked to take over his role. I rigorously analyzed the financials of the company and realized that Cresvale was spending more than they were making! I predicted that they were going to go broke, which they ultimately did. So at that point I needed to take my futures and options group and leave or the group would fall apart. That's how I got to Refco, where my trading group is today.

Q: Tell me about your trading group.

Arlene: We have anywhere between 45 and 55 traders. The reason I say anywhere between is because . . .

Q: You are constantly adding and subtracting traders?

Arlene: We're in Hong Kong, Singapore, Amsterdam, Paris, London, New York, Chicago, and San Francisco. We trade everything.

Q: What do you trade in terms of derivatives?

Arlene: We trade futures and options. We trade cash basis, we trade OTC options, and we trade equity indices.

Q: What do you look for in a trader?

Arlene: I'm not sure if it's anything that you could write down in a formula. You look for confidence, you look for a certain type of experience, a certain presence. You want someone who is knowledgeable and has been around. I tend to only hire experienced traders with proven track records. I'm not interested in taking on junior traders, only in very rare circumstances.

Q: So there's no Sharpe ratio or specific indicator for identifying who is going to be successful.

Arlene: There's no secret formula! It's just sitting and talking with the traders and after you meet—I probably see 150 to 200 traders a year, over a four- or five-year period—after meeting that many traders you just get a sense of who is going to make it.

Q: An intuition?

Arlene: Bob, it's like your book, *The Intuitive Trader.* You get a good sense that you can rely on.

Q: Thanks for the plug.

Arlene: You get a very accurate sense of what makes a good trader tick, who is going to be the right person. Usually I pick right, but like anything else, sometimes I'm wrong too.

Q: Can you think of an example where you really picked right or where you may have really misjudged?

Arlene: Once I hired a proprietary group over the telephone. The head trader left his job where he had been trading for nine years. I hired him without ever meeting him. He has been making a 400 percent return each year on the money that he's been using. The group is extremely profitable. That was just a real winning pick!

Q: Any disasters?

Arlene: Of course. You know, you can't be in this business and not have disasters. I guess my worst trade was when I took on someone who within a week and a half lost all the money that he was supposed to lose ever! I had to let him go. It was a week and a half and it was a lot of money and I was just wrong.

Q: You cut your loss quickly?

Arlene: Oh, yeah.

Q: On to the next trade.

Arlene: Yes.

Q: He didn't bleed you to death.

Arlene: No. But even in a case like that you get a sense of the people who aren't going to work out. As soon as I have that intuition—they could even be up money—I have to let them go just like a trade.

The interesting thing about our business is it's so black and white. There is very little gray. There's no room for someone who is not producing. I may like him, he may be a nice guy, but ultimately it's only about the numbers at the bottom of a piece of paper. And if those numbers don't add up, I don't care how much I like someone. It isn't going to work!

Q: Arlene, you head one of the most profitable proprietary trading groups in the world. Why do you think you're so good at what you do?

Arlene: You meet people on the street all the time and after you get to know them, you can tell exactly what they're suited for. This is just something that totally suits me. Maybe it comes from being a trader. I have a good sense of what my traders want, and as I said, an intuitive ability to give them what they need when they're doing well and letting them go when they're not measuring up.

Q: What do you think traders want?

Arlene: They want a boss who does what she says and delivers what she promises. They want a fair deal and enough capital to trade. They want someone who knows what she's doing, not someone who just takes a piece of paper and says, the numbers are supposed to be in this box and this number is outside the box so you can't make this transaction. They want someone who understands them as traders and their positions and is there to talk to them when they get it right or when they get it wrong.

Q: What does the usual deal look like?

Arlene: A typical deal ranges from the trader taking anywhere from 40 percent to 80 percent of the P&L (profit and loss). Of course a lot depends on his track record and any draws or salaries that he may want.

Q: You raised an interesting point a moment ago. You were saying that after you meet traders for awhile, you have a sense about the person, that you can rely on him or her.

Arlene: Right, after you get to know them. Every time you trade, you can't make money. You have to have losers. It's no different when you hire traders. You're going to have people that don't make money with all the best efforts in the world. My job is to distinguish between the good traders who are having a bad run and the bad trader I don't want to keep!

Q: Arlene, do you think great trading is more of a natural gift or a learned skill?

Arlene: You can learn trading discipline. And of course, traders must be disciplined! You can also learn to have a specific perspective on the market. What you can't learn is when to say, "buy them" on that thousand lot and when to say "buy them" and only do ten contracts. And in my opinion, that marks the difference between an average trader and a great trader. Knowing when to step up to the plate and embrace the extra risk. I don't think that that's something that can be taught.

I mean, you can probably pick up a trader and, with the right training, make him an adequate performer as you can put a tennis racket in a kid's hand and make him a good club player. But, you cannot make him another Andre Agassi!

Q: What you are saying is you can provide someone with a songbook if he has a reasonable voice and teach him some useful operatic techniques but you'll never transform him into Luciano Pavarotti.

Arlene: Of course not. There's something there that makes the difference between being good and being great—the difference between someone who is adequate and the trader who stands out!

Q: Did you have a defining moment in your own trading career?

Arlene: I would say that I did.

Q: Can you talk about it? You're smiling.

Arlene: What I found in life is that you walk down this path. You go this way for all of your life and each day is just like the day before and then every once in awhile a small coincidence occurs in your life and it changes everything forever, personal and professional. This small coincidence that occurred in my life occurred when I decided to stop trading for my own account.

Q: That small coincidence has turned out to be rather large when you look back at it?

Arlene: Yes, it has. So let me tell you about the defining moment that changed me from being a trader to what I do now.

I was home because again I had decided to stop trading and I was reading an article in a futures-and-options publication. I was about to throw it in the rubbish bin. I had it in my hand and my husband was sitting on the couch. And I said, "Maybe you should read this article, dear." It was an article about moving to Australia where the exchange was willing to get you all your papers and provide you with a seat if you would just go down there and make a market.

Q: I remember that.

Arlene: So I showed it to my husband and he said, "Why don't you contact the woman who wrote the article?" Her name is Barbara Diamond. I contacted her and she said, "I don't think Australia is right for you. However, you clear through First Options. Why don't you go see the guys there? They're looking for a broker in England. So I follow Barbara's advice, I go see the guys at First Option, they hire me, I move to London, and my entire life changes! All from the decision to show my husband an article that I was throwing into the garbage bin. That was the defining moment in my trading career!

Q: Do you think trading has had a negative effect on your marriage?

Arlene: Well, it did in my first marriage. It ended it! But I'm very fortunate today that my husband understands the pressure that I'm under and the hours that I work.

Q: Was it the stress of trading that affected your first marriage?

Arlene: The pressure and the fact that my husband couldn't deal with the fact that we would go places and everyone wanted to know about trading and I would get all the attention. In the beginning I can honestly say I was obsessed with trading. I thought about it and talked about it almost all the time, probably for about the first two years.

Q: Was that part of your competitive nature?

Arlene: Probably.

Q: Arlene, you spoke before about relying on your intuition. I've got a pretty good nose myself for identifying traders who have what it takes. I can tell you must have been a pretty good trader just from observing how you process information.

Arlene: Yeah, I was all right. I was pretty good. But honestly you didn't know if you were good because everybody was the same then. The markets were young and we were all learning.

Q: But I can see you always loved the game by your enthusiasm. Do you know who Don Sliter is? He's the single largest independent S&P trader on the floor. He'll do between 3,000 and 5,000 contracts a day. He does very well! When I interviewed Don, one of the things that came through was just this incredible spirit of enthusiasm that was fighting to get out with each answer, and I'm seeing that with you also. As I'm asking the questions, I can just see how much passion you bring to what you do.

Arlene: I love it. What can I say?

Q: And that really comes through! Do you think traders are different from other people?

Arlene: I don't know if they start out different, but they certainly become different.

Q: What do you mean?

Arlene: I think traders become different for a couple of reasons. First of all, it's a very high paying field. So the money makes them different. In my trading group, I've got 29-year-old kids who are going to walk away this year with a million and a half plus dollars, when their friends think it's a big deal to make $50,000. Even if you try not to let the money affect your ego, you become different. You view yourself as different. Also, there's the instant gratification and the competitiveness that you feel in the pit.

Q: So, how do you deal with the 29-year-old kid who is making a million and a half plus dollars a year?

Arlene: One of the things that I pride myself on is not having an ego about this business. Having a big ego about trading is a recipe for disaster. It's what will make a trader lose every penny he's made. If I find a trader in the group who has a big ego, I immediately let them go. I don't care how much money they're making. You can tell by watching how they're trading. They'll get stubborn about a position. They'll think that they're right and the market is wrong! The market is never wrong; the market is always right!

But you can see their ego in other things as well. You see it in their habits and possessions. They drive Ferraris. They wear gold Rolexes! They live in outlandish houses. They fly the Concorde. I don't want traders who do this. I want traders who respect the market and keep their personal egos in check.

Q: Arlene, what was your best moment in the market?

Arlene: My best moment was in London over the ERM (European Rate Mechanism) crisis. I had a trader who was sitting with an awful position. I analyzed our risk and realized this trader was going to lose $10 million to $15 million. I spoke to him. He was a young trader and needed encouragement. I went on the floor with him. He stepped in the pit and at the end of the day, he broke even. That was the most rewarding experience in my trading career.

Q: Do traders feel more alive?

Arlene: I think they're more emotional due to the highs and lows of the market. I used to always say having a good day on the trading floor was better than sex, because you have that ultimate high of the money, of winning, of being better than your peers. And there's nothing, nothing like that feeling! But when you have a bad day, you feel worse than most people. If you're in the advertising industry, you can put together a project and you won't know the results of it for six months. By the time you find out the results, so many things come up that it doesn't have the same emotional impact. In trading, your whole sense of self-worth can be determined by how you did that day.

So I don't know if traders are more alive, but they're certainly more emotional.

Q: Arlene, what has trading taught you about yourself?

Arlene: It has taught me that I can deal with the stress because I'm in my late 40s and I'm still involved with the market and I love it! I've learned that I like the emotional highs and lows and that I'm suited to deal with them.

Q: Arlene, what do you think distinguishes you from everybody else?

Arlene: I had a plan. I visualized what I wanted my career to be. I was focused and I set out to do it and I got lucky. And I grabbed onto each piece of luck that was presented to me and did the most with it. And I'm good at what I do.

Q: I've found the most competent people tend to be the luckiest. Don't you?

Arlene: I focus and I know what I want. I've always known. I have never been one of those people who says, "Oh, I don't know what I want to do with my life or what I want to be." I've known. And I've always known the steps to take and it would take hard work, commitment, and discipline. A lot of people say, "I want to be president of the United States," but they don't know how to go from where they are now to sitting in the White House! I've always known the steps and was willing to pay the price.

You have to be lucky, but then it comes down to your own abilities, you have to know what you're doing, to face the competition and be there to win!

CHAPTER 15

The Comeback Kid

Jerry Letterman

Mr. Letterman is a member of the Index and Options Market of the Chicago Mercantile Exchange. He has been a floor trader, trading his own account for over a decade.

Q: What first attracted you to trading?

Jerry: When I was younger, I used to gamble. I loved the excitement of gambling. I bet on everything. I met Barry Lind (of Lind-Waldock) at my family's country club. He said, "Come down to the exchange." I started as a runner on the trading floor and that's pretty much how I got involved in trading.

Q: Did you make money when you gambled?

Jerry: I did pretty well when I was a kid.

Q: What did you play mostly?

Jerry: Cards, the racetrack. I liked the action.

Q: It's not uncommon for traders to have had an early interest in gambling, but as you know, trading and gambling are not the same thing!

Jerry: I was working on the trading floor as a runner for just a short time when I had a serious car accident. I broke my back and was almost completely paralyzed. So, obviously, I could no longer continue as a runner. I got some money from my insurance company and began trading everything from gold to T-bills to orange juice. On my first or second trade I caught the orange juice and I bought a DeLorean with the profits.

Q: What year was that?

Jerry: The early 80s. I think it was 1981.

Q: Actually, I remember that orange juice trade very well because the Lind-Waldock trading room at the time was all abuzz about some novice who just bought a new car on his first trade in the O.J.

Jerry: I did OK on that trade!

Q: So, in the beginning, were they all winners?

Jerry: No. But I did have a lot of winners early on in my trading. You know, maybe it was beginner's luck. I remember I held a gold position overnight and the next morning it was limit up. I remember once carrying a large position in the T-bills over the weekend and the following Monday the market opened sharply higher. In truth, I didn't really know what I was doing!

Q: At this time were you approaching the market as a gambler or as a trader?

Jerry: As I said earlier I was a kid, 22 years old, and I really didn't know anything. I was just doing it for the excitement.

Q: So, what happened then?

Jerry: My health was improving and I began to study some of the technical aspects of trading. I started to read about charting. At this time the Mercantile Exchange was starting a new program to increase trade volume for some of its less liquid contracts. I leased a seat and began to trade CDs, feeder cattle, and lumber.

Q: Pork bellies?

Jerry: I tried a little of everything in those days. My goal was to develop a trading style and to learn everything I could about the market.

Q: What were you doing on the trading floor?

Jerry: Just trying to make a living! I was single, living downtown, and just tried to learn as much as I could about floor trading. Every year I progressed and I started to make some serious money. I loved the lifestyle! I started getting into some bad habits. I would work an hour or two a day and then go play!

Q: Do you think there was anything in your background that prepared you for trading?

Jerry: I was the Junior Illinois state golf champion at 14. And believe me I was a cocky kid. I had a little money for someone my age and I was very flamboyant. At the time I wanted fast cars and a fast-lane life!

Q: Jerry, talk a little bit about that because as you started making money from trading you got caught up in that, didn't you?

Jerry: I did. In those days there was the drug scene and the clubs, you know, the fast life I was talking about. I was still too young or too stupid to realize there is a day of reckoning when all this stuff catches up with you.

Q: Jerry, what do you think is your key to success in trading?

Jerry: Basically, staying out of big trouble when the markets get volatile; always trying to cut down losses and ride the good ones; just constantly working on my feel and my discipline.

Q: You trade the S&P every day?

Jerry: Right.

Q: Give me a sense of what you are thinking about on the trading floor and what you are trying to do?

Jerry: In the morning session, I try to start off—always operating within disciplined parameters—by watching what the S&P cash and the bonds are doing. At these levels following the order flow is tricky!

Q: What do you think is your greatest strength as a trader?

Jerry: Discipline. I make money 80 percent of the time.

Q: Eighty percent of your trades are winners?

Jerry: On a daily basis, yes. I would say most successful floor traders are making money 70 percent to 80 percent of the time, whether it's $500 dollars or $20,000 on a daily basis. I'm not interested in being one of the traders who swing their equity wildly up and down. I want to grind it out day in and day out. At this stage in my life, I don't have the speed that I did when I was in my 20s in terms of just getting trades. It's a young man's game. It's very athletic, very fast. Let's face it, the S&P is the fastest ball game in the world.

Q: Are you consistent?

Jerry: Most of the time. I make money four out of five days in a week. Yes, overall I would say I do pretty well!

Q: Jerry, what effect do you think trading has had on your marriage?

Jerry: In my opinion, commodity trading and marriage is a very hard combination. I've been on both ends of the success ladder. It's very stressful! I mean I've seen and had it all. I've lived in the million-dollar house, then had tax problems and lost everything! It's very tough. I was divorced, lost all my material possessions, and then woke up one morning and asked myself literally, "What happened?" What did I do wrong, because everything collapsed on me! I had to come up with answers to change my life, to improve my condition.

Q: What did it feel like waking up and realizing that you had lost everything and that you had to start again?

Jerry: It was very, very painful. I mean, it's still very hard for me to describe what that experience feels like. You're so alienated and alone. You become isolated from family and friends. No one wants to talk to you. People said things like, "He blew all this money, he's a bust out."

Q: People drop you?

Jerry: Right.

Q: I know what that feels like. I had the same experience where my "social friends" abandoned me. It's very painful, isn't it?

Jerry: Right. So after that I didn't have the capital to trade and I got into the real business world.

Q: What did you do?

Jerry: I had a marketing company. We marketed a camera that could preexpose a logo onto any surface. And I also represented this other company, but we got into a hostile takeover situation by a firm out of New York. We ended up in court but finally settled. After that I decided I just had to get back to trading.

I was at rock bottom. It was the worst feeling in the world. I was staying home watching the kids. My (second) wife was working, bringing in a few hundred dollars a week. It was horrible! At this point for me to go out and get a job was not easy. I had no college education. I could do sales, but really did not feel like I had any objectively marketable skills. The one thing I knew I was really good at and enjoyed doing was trading!

Q: And of course, you had already experienced the sweet taste of success.

Jerry: It's much harder to go from the top to the bottom. To know you may have to go from making 30 grand a day to 30 grand a year.

Q: So, how did you get back?

Jerry: Well, I met Doug Girard, who leads a proprietary trading group, a couple of years before I left. We had played ball together and I heard that he backed ex-traders.

Q: That he capitalized traders?

Jerry: Yes, capitalized traders and coached them. Doug had faith in me and took me on. We went through membership together, which was a real nightmare considering what my membership application looked like.

Q: Because you disclosed a bankruptcy?

Jerry: They went through the bankruptcy a hundred times and for some odd reason kept focusing on my boat. Was I hiding it? Did I still own it? Hell, I sold the boat and everything else just to feed my family! What happened to the boat? They always asked me what happened to the boat. I said, "The bank took it." "Gone!" It was a very demoralizing process. But I made a commitment to myself that I was going to do it, no matter how tough or how humiliating it got. I was going to handle it with dignity, because I knew I had to get back to trading! I've always been a straight-up player, so I felt I had nothing to hide.

Q: Jerry, I think a lot of people can learn from your experience and can strongly identify with what you went through. It's important to let other people know that someone can go through the experience that you had with resolve and dignity and come back as strong as he was before.

Jerry: I never had a losing year. Even my worst year, when the shit hit the fan with the government, I made in seven months over $100,000.

Q: That's your worst year?

Jerry: My lifestyle was just too high; I couldn't afford it. So everything had to collapse. What I realize now was it was inevitable.

It had to happen. And I'm lucky that I was given the opportunity to learn from that experience!

I've been through a lot in my life. Sometimes I feel I've been through all the hell life can serve up! You name it, it's happened to me! I broke my back and I was paralyzed, I've been through a tough divorce. I've lost all my money. Friends abandoned me but I came back and you know what I have learned from all this?

Q: What have you learned?

Jerry: I've learned that your family is the most important thing in the world. And as long as you are an honest, disciplined, and straight-up guy, you'll make it in this world! Just be true to yourself and your code, and things will come together.

Q: Jerry, it really sounds like you've got it together!

Jerry: I'm fortunate. Things have really gone great since I've come back.

Q: You said earlier that, when you first started trading, what appealed to you was the electricity and action of the market, the gambling aspect of trading. Does that still hold any attraction for you?

Jerry: Not at all. I haven't gambled on football or sports since I got back. I don't treat trading as gambling. The discipline I learned is this is a business. I come in each day to make a living.

Q: So for you it has been a complete attitudinal change?

Jerry: Just come down to the exchange and take what the market gives you. It has nothing at all to do with excitement or gambling. Take what you can and minimize your losses.

Q: What, in your opinion, is a good floor trader?

Jerry: A good trader is an honest trader—someone who steps out and turns the market or makes a trade without getting spoon fed by a broker. Someone who is a market maker in the true sense.

Q: And is willing to embrace the risk?

Jerry: Yes, embrace the risk and take the consequence no matter what.

Q: Do you think traders are different from other people?

Jerry: Most traders are high-strung. I'm kind of a high-strung person myself. I'll give you an example. When I'm in the real world . . .

Q: Oh, trading is not the real world?

Jerry: Well, let's say I go out with another couple and I'm at a restaurant, I'm very demanding! If I want service or a check, they go, Jerry, what's the rush? You know, being in the market, I'm used to fast, immediate "service."

Q: And it's not necessarily that you're being rude, it's just that you live in this frenetic world, and you want things when you want them and you don't want delays.

Jerry: That's correct. I want service!

Q: So how does that work out when you're with other people? Do they understand that?

Jerry: They feel kind of intimidated and probably ask, "What's going on with this guy?" They don't know me.

Q: They don't know that you really are a nice guy?

Jerry: I guess it rubs off from trading all my life. They say, "Jerry, you're so hyper." "Where are you going?" "Slow down, relax."

Q: Based on everything you have told me and learned about yourself, if you went in tomorrow and made a million dollars what effect would it have on you?

Jerry: The best moment I ever had in the market was the '87 crash. I made tons of money. It was great. I was on top of the world. I was 27 years old and made an overnight fortune. I went to New York, stayed in the finest hotels, took limos, wined and dined, and bought jewelry. I spent a lot of money and had a great time.

But if I made a million dollars tomorrow, I would not reenact that scene. I'd put the money under lock and key and not spend a single penny of it! I truly know now that I can handle the peaks and the valleys. So I just try and keep things on a stable line. I don't allow myself to get in trouble.

In the old days I'd get on an airplane, go anywhere in the world, eat at the finest restaurants. I don't do that anymore! I'm strictly a family man who loves to hang out with my children. I go to work and make a living and take it one day at a time.

Q: What distinguishes Jerry Letterman from all the other traders?

Jerry: I say what I mean and I'm up front. There's no bullshit. I believe in integrity and I'm not afraid of being who I am. My father, who I was very close to, died a few years ago. It was at the same time I was hitting bottom. He used to say to me, "Be a man. Have integrity. Be straight up. No matter how tough life gets, you'll be OK." Now I know what he means!

CHAPTER 16

West of Eden

David Lansburgh

Mr. Lansburgh is a member of the International Monetary Market. He is a floor trader specializing in the Swiss franc.

Q: David, what first attracted you to trading?

David: Initially, I heard about trading through a friend of mine in Miami who knew somebody who was a member of the Chicago Mercantile Exchange. He thought trading suited my personality.

Q: What was it about your personality that he thought made you suitable for trading?

David: I think just being outgoing and aggressive, having a good head on my shoulders, and being a little crazy! My friend said that the trader in Chicago would let me work for him for the summer. He told me I'd get to work on the trading floor. I thought, okay, sounds great. I'm always up for new ideas.

Q: What were you doing before that?

David: I was in college at the University of Texas.

Q: Did you enjoy school?

David: Yeah. I liked the University of Texas a lot—lots of fun. I was thinking of going to law school or graduate school. I was kind of lost and didn't know what I wanted to do.

Q: So you came up to Chicago after school?

David: Actually, between my junior and senior year. So I walked into this trader's office, I didn't know one person in the whole city of Chicago, and this guy who I was told was a big-time Chicago trader comes out wearing a Bozo the Clown shirt with a purple and pink tie.

Q: He was a local?

David: Yes. I introduced myself and called him mister and he cracked up and started laughing. He says, "Mister, that's my father. Call me by my first name. Don't ever call me that again!" That was the beginning of a great summer. I think I worked one hour that day. We had breakfast for an hour and then we were on the golf course for the rest of the day.

Q: Which market were you working in?

David: S&Ps.

Q: What were you doing?

David: I was checking his positions, counting his cards, picking up his dry cleaning, you name it! I loved the activity of the markets. It was very exciting. It was a very stimulating atmosphere.

Q: What was it that you found so stimulating?

David: The money, the thirst, the action, the hours, the lifestyle!

Q: David, do you think there was anything in your background that prepared you for trading?

David: I think my childhood was pretty unique. I grew up in Miami. My family was in the hotel business. We owned the Eden Roc and a number of other hotels on the beach. It was pretty exciting and a little unusual. I was in a pretty high energy atmosphere as a kid.

Q: David, was that one of the things that first attracted you to trading, the fact that it is a high-profile profession and has its own electricity?

David: No.

Q: No?

David: No. I really didn't know what I was getting into until I actually came up to Chicago. I had no idea what trading was all about, I think like most people who think they know something about trading and then they get on the floor and they're lost. They realize that they have no idea how it works or what it's really all about!

Q: So how did you get started?

David: Well, I knew I loved trading from the first couple of days I was down on the trading floor. Just the flurry of activity and everything. So I told my dad I wanted to go to Chicago and become a professional trader. I started as a runner for Bear Stearns, just running orders in and out of the trading pits.

Q: Were you working in any particular location or on the floor?

David: I was in the foreign currency quadrant. While I was running, I watched the markets very carefully and would get gut feelings of where to buy and sell the currencies.

Q: What was your first trade like?

David: There was nothing like that first day! Walking on the trading floor! I was lost and very excited all at the same time!

Q: Was it a rush?

David: It was a huge rush—intense. I made $287.50. Believe me, it was the most exciting day of my life. It was great!

Q: What made it so great?

David: There was a lot of anxiety leading up to that day. I remember walking to work that morning after not sleeping the whole night before. I was very nervous. You know, you're in the pit with 100 seasoned traders. You're a new face.

Q: What were you nervous about?

David: I just wanted to do well. I was starting a whole new career. I wanted to perform well.

Q: So you made $287.50 your first day. Pretty good. It's better than most new traders make on their first day.

David: It was great.

Q: David, do you think in the long run it was to your advantage that you made money on your first day of trading?

David: I don't know if it was to my advantage, but I decided I was going to trade small for a long time until I felt comfortable. I had a system that I developed with a trader who has been a market maker for 25 years. He was my mentor.

Q: Who is he?

David: Mark Markham.

Q: Oh, I know Mark. I used to stand next to him when I first started trading on the floor. He's a good trader.

David: Yeah, he's a good trader. Mark and I started meeting every day for breakfast before the markets opened. I think he wanted to help me and I also feel I helped him. He had been whacked around a few times. He kind of wanted to go back to get disciplined and get a fresh look. I think he viewed me as someone he could kind of start over with. In a very positive way, we fed off each other. He had all the knowledge and I had all the youth and enthusiasm. I think he saw me as a young talent.

Q: You had the energy and the desire . . .

David: And the discipline Mark was looking for. He had a system. It was an opening range system that he swore by but he was having a hard time executing. He told me it was the simplest system, but the best on the floor. So I just started trading it every day. I had no hesitation or fear. I believed in it and it worked. It still does to this day.

Q: Makes money every day?

David: Not every day, but in the long run, you're going to make money using it. You just need the discipline and the confidence to execute.

Q: Is it a break-out system?

David: It's a break-out system where you try to catch market direction. If it trades above the opening range, you get long. If it goes below the opening range, you get short. And if it goes to the opening range . . .

Q: You watch out!

David: That's right. If it goes two or three times into the range, you don't trade for the rest of the day because you'll get chopped up. In the currencies you'll catch a move for 100 points without any risk at all!

Q: David, what do you think in your background prepared you for trading?

David: I think sports definitely has had a lot to do with my success at trading. I was always a very good athlete. I'm very competitive.

Q: What sport?

David: I was a nationally ranked tennis player for ten years. I used to travel all around the country playing in tournaments. I think trading is very much like a game. When people ask me what makes you good at trading, I think it is the same qualities and attributes that you need to be successful at sports. I definitely think that having a history of success in competitive athletics is a huge advantage. Trading is a game. You are competing against other traders and you're competing against yourself.

Q: How so?

David: I just feel like the discipline is to trade the market. I don't let other traders affect what I do. Obviously, if I see certain things happen I react. But I just stick to my focus and exploit whatever the market gives me. I'm trading against the market, realizing it has to be given respect all the time.

Q: David, do you think your trading was more of a learned skill or a natural talent?

David: In my case, it was definitely a natural talent.

Q: I've seen you trade on the floor. You're very focused. I can see you're disciplined and you also know how to let go.

David: I feel I'm very fortunate. I just picked it up. It has been very natural for me. I think I'm blessed to have the exact qualities that totally fit this business.

Q: What do you think those qualities are in a nutshell?

David: I think the keys to success in trading are discipline, intuition, good instincts, and being aggressive–knowing when you're wrong, to have the discipline to move. You can't have any opinions. I never have an opinion! People always ask me, what do you think? The less I think, the better I'll do. Just focus on the market's action and respond!

Q: Did you have a defining moment in your trading career? Did you ever have either a great trade or you went through a down period where you just learned something that kind of changed the way you approached the market?

David: I have been extremely fortunate in my career. I have never really had a drawdown for more than a month or so. Sometimes I may go a couple of weeks where the market is slow or I get in a trading slump but there has never been a prolonged period of loss for me.

Q: That's pretty exceptional!

David: I've never had two losing months in a row! Maybe I have one losing month a year. But let me tell you about a good trade that I had. It's probably the best day trade I ever made. I sold 200 contracts of Swiss francs and as I sold them the Fed made an announcement. I think they raised rates. The market started breaking. It was down 100 points and I was short 200 contracts.

Q: That's a quarter of a million!

David: It was a great feeling. The market just collapsed. In truth, if I would have shut up for another two minutes, I would have even been better off. I wish I had a little laryngitis for a minute so I wouldn't have bought my position back that quickly.

Q: Did you celebrate?

David: I had a party with my friends.

Q: David, what does it feel like, being in your 20s, making incredible sums of money? How do you deal with it? As you know a lot of people just can't handle it.

David: I think many traders in this business don't come from money. And when they start making big money—it comes fast and plentifully—they don't know how to deal with it! Fortunately, I grew up in a family that was quite substantial. I was always taught the value of a dollar and I was ingrained from an early age that you have to work hard to make a buck. So, although initially I was excited with the winnings, I've never really been an extravagant person.

It's not really the money that I like, it's more the game. It's knowing that I'm good and doing the best I can do. I know it hasn't affected my personality. I'm still the same person I was before I started trading.

Q: What is your greatest strength as a trader?

David: I'm very disciplined and very instinctive. I have a great feel for the markets and know how to keep out of trouble. I'm also very patient, which is a very good quality for being a trader. You don't want to trade when the market's not there. If the market doesn't offer an opportunity, you must be prepared to sit on the sidelines and wait for an opening. That definitely is a skill that I have acquired over time; I didn't have it initially.

Q: Being patient?

David: Yes. Being more discriminating about trades. There are many times I will just watch the market and not trade until I see an opportunity.

Q: Which is to say you've developed a better sense of when you think your strategy has a high probability of being successful?

David: Absolutely. Yes.

Q: What do you look for?

David: I look at the order flow, the volume, and I follow the Deutsche mark. I find it often leads the way and is a good barometer for direction.

Q: David, let's change subjects. What effect has trading had on your relationships?

David: I've never had too many love relationships but in general, I would have to say it has been good for my relationships. I get to go meet a wide range of people, spend time with my friends, and travel wherever and whenever I want to.

Q: What about stress?

David: People ask me all the time, "How do you handle the stress of being a floor trader?" Honestly, I really don't have any stress from trading! Granted, there are certain days where the trading just gets to me and I want to go home and take time off when I don't want to be with anybody else. But those days are far and few between and have very little to do with the way I approach trading. In actuality, I get energized.

Q: It's exciting like a competitive sport?

David: It's exactly like being in a game or playing a tournament. When I leave the trading floor, you can't tell if I made or lost money for the day. It doesn't affect my moods and I don't take it out on other people.

Q: So you've learned to keep it in perspective?

David: Yeah. I try to have a very balanced attitude about what I'm doing. In fact that's one of the ways I'm able to stay on the top of my game!

It's fascinating to be among all the different players who make up the traders on the exchange floor. Each trading pit seems to have its own unique personality and within each pit there is a colorful array of personalities with interesting backgrounds and perspectives.

Q: Speaking of keeping things in perspective, what was your worst moment in the market?

David: I don't remember all the gory details but I lost a considerable amount of money on one trade.

Q: Do you remember how much you lost?

David: I lost $135,000.

Q: That's a bad day!

David: Yes. That was a very bad day!

Q: What did it feel like going home with that kind of loss?

David: Making a lot of money in one day is a very intense feeling, but losing a lot of money in a day is a much worse feeling even when you're trying to keep the whole thing in perspective. I was feeling kind of miserable. You've been there, Bob, you can understand what I'm saying.

Q: Absolutely. I've experienced that a number of times.

David: So, at the same time I'm telling myself to keep this whole thing in balance because in reality I could afford the loss, I'm still feeling miserable. I went home and slept all day and I will have to say the feeling carried over for a few days. But then, you know, you compose yourself and get back to basics and realize it's just another game or another tournament, and it's your responsibility to be prepared and that means having a mental edge.

Q: How do you compose yourself?

David: You have to put the emotion and intensity of the loss behind you and look at the big picture. Analyze why you tripped up and go back to basics that brought you success in the first place. For me, I just keep reminding myself of what I am capable of doing. And when I'm back on the trading floor I don't try to force anything, I just trade the market and start fresh.

Q: What do you mean by "going back to the basics?"

David: I Just say the same things to myself that I always did. Be disciplined and be focused. When I walk to work in the morning I put myself through, let's call it, a "mental warm up." I say to myself over and over again, "Be disciplined, trade the market, stick and move!" These are just reminders to myself before I get on the trading floor to get myself psychologically prepared to be a winner.

Q: You are pumping yourself up?

David: Yes, just to pump myself up and remind myself that each trading day is like the bottom of the ninth, three-two count.

I think it's good to be pumped, but you don't want to be overly excited because sometimes then you're going to do things in a quiet market where there's no movement. So in these situations you don't want to get too excited or aggressive. This is when the real art of trading comes in. You also have to psyche yourself to be patient. That's why trading is so tough. It's all about fine-tuning your own attitudes and motivations.

Q: David, do you have a role model?

David: When I first started trading in the Swiss franc pit there was a guy I stood next to for the first couple of years. His name was Mike Ansani. Do you remember him?

Q: I remember him very well.

David: I think he was a great trader. Always sticking and moving, buying and selling—kind of reminds me of myself now.

Q: Traded large size.

David: Yes, he traded very large size and always made a two-sided market.

The only thing he lacked, because he clearly had a great feel for the markets, was discipline. He ended up losing millions of dollars in just a couple of days. But he was a guy that I looked up to and said, "God, this guy is good." And what I meant was he had great instincts and trading mechanics!

Q: So you were able to take from him his best trading qualities and reject his worst?

David: Exactly. Because as I said earlier, I've always been very disciplined. I've never had any trouble with that.

Q: When you are carrying a large position, how do you trade it? Do you usually sell it all at once or do you piece it out?

David: It all depends. If I get on a big position and it's a winner, then I scalp out of it.

Q: All at once?

David: No. If I buy 100 contracts, I'll start selling 20 at a time as long as it's going my way. If it's a loser, I'm looking to dump all of it as quick as possible! If I'm wrong, that's what I want to do. I want to hit the first bid and sell as many as I can. I won't hold positions for a long time that are going against me.

Q: What do you like most about trading?

David: I like the action. I still get a rush from the trade when it's busy and we're rocking and rolling. When the markets are moving, it's just fun. It's a fantastic game. That's what I like about it!

Q: What has trading taught you about yourself?

David: As with any sport, trading definitely brings out people's true personalities, I think you really get to see what you are made of. As far as I'm concerned, I consider myself to be a very upstanding trader. I'm reminded daily to value all the things that I was taught as a child: to be honest, disciplined, and hardworking. For me, in a lot of ways, trading is a constant character test.

It frustrates me many times to see some of the things that go on down there. You know, you'll run into people on the street and they will say, "Oh, that guy has made millions down on the floor." And I'm saying to myself, That guy is such a piece of shit! I mean, he's a dirtbag and he stole all his money. Personally, I wouldn't be able to sleep at night if I did those kinds of things.

Q: What do you think distinguishes you from everyone else?

David: I think there are a lot of good traders, but I just think I have a unique feel for the market and for the size that I trade. A lot of people tend to freeze up when they take on big positions, and don't handle it as well. I can trade 100 lots like I do one lot. It's the discipline that allows me to do everything else!

Q: Do you enjoy trading more than running the Eden Roc?

David: Yes, I do. Although I will have to say it was pretty good, totally stress free.

Q: Free swimming pool and tennis court.

David: Free food, free access to the restaurants whenever I wanted. It was a good life!

Q: But you love trading more?

David: Yes, I love trading. There's nothing in the world like it. When we're busy and the adrenaline is rushing: Give me one place in the world where I want to be and it's right here!

CHAPTER 17

Tom's Edge

Tom Grossman

Mr. Grossman is president of SAC International Equities, LLC.
He was formerly the head foreign equities trading
strategist for Kingdon Capital Management.

Q: Tom, what first attracted you to trading?

Tom: I think the immediate feedback, being able to know fairly quickly the value of your opinion. In trading, you get feedback of all kinds. It's a continual learning process and no other occupation that I know offers such immediate feedback when you're right or when you're wrong.

Q: How did you get involved in trading?

Tom: I was in college, bumbling along, and met a finance professor who was a very interesting man. He worked three days a week as a money manager for an investment firm in Manhattan. Using my math skills, I was allowed to aid in his strategies. Today a lot of the stuff that he was doing is very commonplace and can be found in every piece of software around. But at that point doing collars and some of the stuff that ultimately became the maligned portfolio insurance-type stuff was cutting edge.

At this point I was just working on these strategies. I didn't directly implement them into the market, but certainly saw the returns through my professor's money management firm. As a result of this experience I got friendly with some option brokers and managed to weasel out a job for myself in 1988, which was no easy feat right after the crash!

Q: Where did you end up landing a job?

Tom: I got a job at what was then Shearson, Lehmann, Hutton, on the options desk in the retail special-handling area. It was a fascinating job to have because I was trading options for retail brokers who were handling wealthy individual clients throughout the country. So you had rich guys with industry knowledge trading in different parts of the country. For example, you had people in the Silicon Valley trading technology stocks. It was a time for takeovers like UAL and Hilton Hotels. It was one of the best living case studies I could imagine for getting a first-hand look at the fear and greed of trading.

Q: What was so fascinating?

Tom: I think it was just the game itself. It was the hunt, if you will. Seeing what made money and what were the classical errors, just really thinking about the whole investment process and how many different and interesting ways there were to go about it. Just learning about what worked to make money consistently in the markets and what strategies and tactics meshed with my personality.

Q: Do you think there was anything in your background that prepared you for trading?

Tom: Yes, definitely. Sports and gambling, which were a big part of my life when I was growing up. Particularly the sports, which I played all through college.

Q: What did you play?

Tom: In high school I played football and lacrosse and I was also a swimmer. In college, I concentrated exclusively on football. I certainly think the competitive element, the discipline involved in succeeding at sports, spills over to most occupations, but trading particularly.

I mentioned gambling. My father has always been a gambler in one way or another and I accompanied him to the racetrack for most of my life. And so from an early age I really felt that I knew what I was doing. I developed a real "feel" for fear and greed and probabilities, also the joy of gaining an edge and being correct. I know of no one in the world who displays that joy more often or with more enthusiasm than my father. I really fed off that high!

Q: It's really interesting that you mention sports and gambling, because that seems to be a recurring theme with many of the traders I've interviewed. It is a strong part of their background. But as you know, the skills that you employ both in sports and gambling can be a double-edged sword. I was wondering, in terms of your initial foray into trading, what were the positive and negative influences of your background experiences?

Tom: I think in retrospect, I was fortunate that my father was a good gambler. I learned by watching him that most people don't know how to play. It's the difference between being a player and being a loser. Most people go to the track or to a casino to get some kind of high, to get a mood change. Or they play to make a quick killing, which is the antithesis of what I would consider "good playing." For others it becomes very expensive entertainment! In retrospect, what was fascinating to me then and still is in my current business is just the joy of gaining an edge over everyone else; not focusing on the end result, the money. I think for me that's the key, to get that edge, whether it's reading the racing form better than the others or maybe feeling that because of your understanding of sports, you can dissect the psychological mood of a team. Knowing when you really have an edge is an art form. When I went to the track with my father, I can tell you that sometimes on a winning bet he would fully handicap 40 races before he would place a bet. But when he felt like he had one, the joy he had parading around with that advantage in his mind! The time before the race was more elating to him than the actual victory. Clearly, it was gratifying for him when it did work out, but the emotion of having the edge and knowing he waited patiently for the winner to present itself was a huge high. I think focusing on the process instead of the result has been a significant help for me in trading.

Q: I guess that's what you meant earlier when you said the attraction for you is the game itself.

Tom: That's right.

Q: When you were working for Shearson, what was the actual trading like?

Tom: To be honest, it was a precursor to really trading. In fact, I was what most people in the world call a trader, but this is really nothing more than an order placement clerk. I was not taking positions.

Q: You were what I call the head on the missile!

Tom: Exactly right. I was clearly that. To use your term, I was riding on someone else's missile! I was not generating any of my own trading positions.

Q: Tom, currently you head a trading desk for Kingdon Capital, which manages about $2 billion. You trade both equities and futures around the world. What is the attraction of trading for you now?

Tom: As I said before, I think it all comes down to feeling like I can get an edge! Of course, the actual trade represents an expression of discipline or a technical overlay to gain that edge. And the edge may be that I'm the only guy who is up trading paper stocks in Indonesia and Scandinavia. On some days I have to pinch myself to make sure that I'm not being pompous and thinking that I have an edge when it is not there. But when I have it, I know how to exploit it. So what still holds my fascination is just constantly proving to myself that my process can identify these situations and make good trades. That's really the joy of what I do. Also the intellectual challenge, all these constantly moving parts across different asset classes in different geographical regions, among a variety of investor groups.

Q: Tom, do you think your trading is more karma or dogma?

Tom: Definitely, more karma.

Q: How do you mean that?

Tom: For me, if I think too dogmatically and begin to posit efficient market arguments, it doesn't allow for the emotional and mental freedom I need for a true edge in the market. I know it may sound arrogant to think that I can figure out a market or have a better feel, but I just know intuitively that you can gain an edge for a time in these markets! I think if you don't go with a karma approach, you never have the confidence or the high level of personal need to be a really successful trader.

Q: So what you're really talking about is what is the central theme of *The Intuitive Trader.* Is that correct?

Tom: Yes. I've read your work on intuition and it's absolutely right. Call it karma or intuition; they're interrelated in my mind.

Early in my career at Kingdon, the Japanese equity market was extremely weak. The Nikkei had broken 15,000 and everyone in the world was bearish. I started to feel on a purely intuitive basis and then later on a more dogmatic or quantitative basis that the market was ready to take off and I built a case for a long position in what was a very illiquid, difficult market to trade. The result, however, was that I picked the bottom of the market and had an extremely profitable trade! And I think that defines my confidence in my own intuition and investment process. You must have the courage of your own convictions to buck the trend and act on your own intuitive beliefs.

Q: Did taking that trade provide you with internal freedom to trade in a way that you hadn't traded before?

Tom: Yes, both from a psychological and process point of view. It was a huge confidence builder for me, and there's really been no turning back since I made that trade. In actuality, I left something out. The trade happened in even a better way. At first, it didn't work out and I needed the discipline to get out and the emotional commitment and confidence to get back into the trade when I thought the timing was right.

Q: Those are the trades that always feel the best, aren't they?

Tom: I think that's right. They shake you up at first but you still know in your heart you're right so you got to get back in. To me, those are always the most gratifying trades. The Nikkei trade gave me confidence because we weren't drawing a line in the sand. We were flexible and we were going to trade along our original thesis, but when the timing was right! It's hard for a lot of psychological reasons to buy something back at a worse price than you bought it the first time. But many times it's a grave error not to.

Q: Personally, I never mind getting out of a trade. But man, do I hate when it goes without me and I'm left standing on the sidelines. That is the worst feeling!

Tom: Absolutely.

Q: What do you believe is your greatest strength as a trader?

Tom: I'd say mental flexibility. I'm not averse to taking anything in the market as an input. Also, understanding that the amount of physical, mental, and emotional effort it takes to build an algorithm is only a temporary thing that you're going to have to fine-tune or throw out! I think working through this process is my greatest strength. You can't be too restrictive in what you look at as an input. Because the obvious ones, everyone is exploiting.

Q: Exactly. It's like what I used to say when I was on the trading floor. Traders or clerks used to come up to me and they'd pump me on a "no-risk" or "low-risk" trade. I'd always say, take it to someone else, I'm not interested. I want the ones that are risky, but I want to be able, obviously, to circumscribe the risk.

Tom: That's right.

Q: I mean, the ones that everybody is seeing as no-risk, usually mean no pay-off, right?

Tom: Or huge risk, because everyone's wrong and it's a crowded trade.

Q: Exactly. Now do you think traders are different from other people? Do you think we process information differently as a group?

Tom: I think again, you have to be careful, at least on the equity side of the business, as to who you define as a trader. In any case, I think true traders are very different in many ways. But the one that comes to mind as the essential difference is constantly holding yourself to a standard of intellectual honesty. I think many professionals are not intellectually honest about the value they add to whatever process they're involved in. A true trader is constantly trying to understand, evaluate, and fine-tune his efforts to be honest about what actions produced what results.

Q: I think along those lines traders are always trying to deconstruct the last trade, aren't they? They're just perpetually trying to simplify and get every action down to its distillate, to make each effort as pure as possible with no bullshit; whether it is a feeling, an intuition, a hesitation, whatever!

Tom: I think that's right. I think that's the difficult process for most people to go through, because it's not how most people operate. So you have to learn how to cultivate that level of introspection, even though it's not a natural thing to do.

Q: How did you learn to do that?

Tom: Ironically, I've never really thought about it as such. But, off the cuff, I'd say it goes back to watching my father at the race track. You know, in horse racing you lose a lot and people say, "Oh, the damn jockey cost me the race" or "I had the best horse but it was a bad track." The smart guys never think of it that way, they look back and analyze the race and the horse that beat them and figure out what they missed.

Q: And if they're really smart, they'll ask themselves why they put money on that one.

Tom: Exactly. And it's the same thing with traders. You're in a trade that you know someone else is in and it blows up and he calls yelling about whatever. "The damn president said this" or you know, you've heard it a million times! The true trader is the guy that views each decision as an opportunity to learn something useful about himself and the market in the process of making profitable trades.

Q: What was your worst moment in the market? Anything stand out?

Tom: There's so many of them. In truth, the bad ones are harder to remember. But the worst ones don't stand out because if you are really disciplined they never get out of hand. Part of the process is that I tend to have a million small losses and small problems. The key is keeping them small!

Q: How do you get through losing periods?

Tom: I get very small in my trades.

Q: You reduce your position size?

Tom: Absolutely. I find at times I'm just out of sync with the market. So I get very small, and when I feel I'm back in sync and feel my trading size is too small, I know that the market has told me something valuable.

Q: Who is your most memorable character during your trading career?

Tom: I'd say Eric Scheinberg at Goldman Sachs. He's a longtime partner. His trading style is different than mine, but he's an unbelievable trader. He's an absolute contrarian. Eric's been in the game day in and day out for 25 to 30 years and is just the most introspective and confident trader that I know.

Q: Can you give an example of that?

Tom: There were ten or eleven times when I was at Goldman Sachs that the stocks that we were heavily involved in were just absolutely getting killed. I remember Eric on one day in particular. There were three huge sellers in one of the stocks. It was getting crushed and was in a free fall for four or five days. I had recognized Eric as a great trader before that and was not alone; of course, that's why he was a partner of the firm. When the noise level would rise, Eric used to stroll out of his office. He just had this amazing sense of, let's call it timing. I would glance at his office when I knew there was an issue and wait for him to walk out. And he would appear and very matter-of-factly inquire, "What's the story?" I think truthfully he knew a lot more of the story than he let on before he'd ask the question.

Q: It reminds me of a friend of mine who was a huge player on the floor of the exchange. We'd be in a position together and the market would be sharply low against us and of course John knew tick for tick where the market was. He would call me up and ask if the market was up or down. Same sort of thing!

Tom: Yeah. And then he would literally make the bottom of these stocks. So he had this great ability to know when to fight the battle and as you know it's a very rare talent, to know how to distinguish between taking a stand and being stubborn.

Q: Do you think traders feel more alive?

Tom: Absolutely. The immediate feedback cycle that attracted me initially to trading makes you feel more alive. Of course this may be a simplification, but there's a very easy measure to determine whether you should be happy or sad at the end of the day. Personally, when I'm interviewing a young trader, I look for him to have an analytical discipline and the ability to have distance from the market, but if someone doesn't demonstrate real excitement for trading, I don't think they'll make it.

Q: That they don't get that jolt of electricity?

Tom: My old boss used to say, if they don't really get a hard-on when they hear a good story, then they're not going to be dedicated enough to work the way that the guys that get that rush do!

Q: I think that metaphor says a lot. There have been so many times I've seen traders with this attitude that's just slightly above lethargy. It's no wonder they're not performing.

Tom: Apparently some traders can be completely dispassionate and are just so disciplined and analytical that they can grind out a very good living from the market.

Q: We're not talking about the dispassion of an analytical temperament. Call it curiosity or interest or state of mind. That level of passion and intellectual challenge has to be present.

Tom: For me, when the markets really get ugly, either very strong or weak or very volatile, I really get juiced. A lot of traders want to step away, to turn off their screen, and not get involved because the human reaction to danger is fear, to shy away.

I view it the other way. The way I see it, you've invested all of this time, emotion, and energy in observing the market and at this moment I'm committed to having a better view and stronger and more decisive reaction than anyone else. I must play the market at those times. Those are the moments I live for!

Q: Tom, it's like your dad at the racetrack, patiently waiting for the right pick then going for it! Looking for that moment when the seams are starting to cut loose, when everyone else is running around like chickens without heads, you are prepared to have a decisive response to the market.

Tom: Absolutely. I find you have to recognize when you have an advantage. If you're not sitting with a position in a market that's getting killed, that's a tremendous advantage because you don't have the emotional pain that everyone else is experiencing. It's almost your duty or responsibility to yourself to play. I say to myself, there are traders in pain here, losing their cars and houses, whatever, and it's time to play. I have to take action. You can smell the blood of other people's losses. That has to kick up on your radar screen, you must seize that advantage. In fact, that's what makes the game worth playing!

Q: I have a very good friend who's a large S&P trader. He trades anywhere from 300 to 500 S&Ps at a time for his personal account. He once told me when he started trading S&Ps he was totally daunted by the market because of its volatility. The way he said it was, the market would take his breath away! And he said he reflected on that fact for a long time and what he came up with was that whenever the market took his breath away, in a literal sense he knew, as a physical and psychological stimulus that he had to get involved. It was in fact, as you say, his responsibility to himself to trade.

Tom: Absolutely. I understand that completely. You have to be in the market long enough to understand what it feels like to have no position, what it feels like for the people with the wrong position or the right position, for that matter; to know even when someone is right, there is a natural tendency to want to get out too soon to appease your psyche and say, look I was right; to be willing to say, even if you're not in the market, you know why they're selling it; and also to not be afraid to buy it even though it's already sharply higher. Ask around, it's not an easy thing to do! Most traders say it's a very dangerous sport trying to pick tops or bottoms. But I think if you do it with discipline, it can be unbelievably rewarding. You're going to be wrong a lot and take a lot of little losses, but when you're right, it's a home run.

Q: It's tough to stick your hand in the fire, but that's what we get paid for, right?

Tom: That's right. If you're quick and disciplined and smart, the opportunities are there. It's like I said before, you have to know when you have the edge and go for it!

Q: What do you think trading has taught you about yourself?

Tom: That's an interesting question. I'm not sure if trading has taught me something about myself or molded me into what I've become.

Q: How would you answer it?

Tom: My gut tells me that trading has taught me about myself.

Q: What has it taught you?

Tom: It's taught me to be constantly honest with myself, that I have an inner confidence that's unshakable, which most traders don't have.

Q: Do you think that came from your background in athletics or do you think it was molded, as you say, by the day-to-day self-analysis that you have to do in your trading?

Tom: I think it really comes down to either you're born with it or it's developed during your childhood. I've certainly been accused of being arrogant more than once during my life. But there is a certain level of self-confidence, I think it is partially due to the way I was brought up and has nothing to do with the emotion of the racetrack, because my dad always taught me about the real danger of the racetrack. I guess I would have to say, whether it was a fistfight in the second grade or playing football or playing the trumpet, which in retrospect I was absolutely horrible at, I was absolutely unquestionably positive that with the right effort I could do better than anyone else!

Q: If you think about it on a philosophical level, the whole act of trading itself is in many ways an arrogant act—to think that you can come to the table and pull off chips on a consistent basis. Paradoxically, there is an underlying feeling of humility that gives you that level of self-confidence.

Tom: I do believe that part of the arrogance that's needed is having no fear of being wrong. I think most traders are just so deathly afraid of being wrong that they can't allow themselves to be right! In the market or in sports when the game is on the line, somebody has got to take the shot! There are four guys on the court thinking, oh, man, it would suck to miss. And then there's one player saying, give me the damn ball, I'm going to make the shot!

Q: Tim McAuliffe, who is a large market maker on the Chicago Mercantile Exchange has a strong background in athletics. He made that same point. Tim said, with three seconds to go, he wants to be the guy who is going to take the last shot; he's not going to pass off. And not only is he not afraid of that situation, but he just loves to be in that position. He may miss, but in his heart he knows no one on the team is going to give a better effort.

Tom: Exactly. I mean, the truth is, with a gun pointed to my head when I'm playing golf, I'm still going to focus on the shot. And in fact I have no right to think of myself as a great putter. Clearly, if it could be measured quantitatively, there are much better putters in the world. But if you put a gun to my head and said make this ten-footer straight up a hill, in my mind no one is going to do a better job than me. Not Tiger Woods or anyone else. Thank you very much, I'll do it myself!

Q: That's exactly what Tim said. He plays golf for money all the time now. He also added, "You do not want to be betting on me to miss a putt." I don't think it's really a question of arrogance. It's much more a strong expression of self-confidence, that he's there to really play the game. And bottom line, he's in control. He's responsible for whatever happens.

Tom: Part of it is, you have to be intellectually honest. I know Tiger Woods practices his putting a lot more than I do and is certainly more gifted physically. But in that moment, knowing what the stakes are and knowing the situation, I still believe I've got a better chance.

Q: What do you think distinguishes you from everyone else?

Tom: I actively search for opportunities that no one else is looking for. And I have the confidence to do the trades, to try them and to know that I'll be wrong a lot. And I have the conviction that overall I'm still going to come out way ahead.

Q: As you said earlier, that's a considerable advantage over everyone else because most traders shy away from coming up to the plate. All they see is the fear or vision of the trade not working out.

Tom: What happens to me a lot of times is I do a great deal of work on a theory or strategy and the actual trade comes down to no value. And unless you derive that pure joy of identifying and getting the edge when it is there for a minute, a day, a week, or a month, then you won't be able to tolerate all the dead ends. As long as that joy is with me I've got to be confident that I'm going to stay at the head of the pack. I know and have seen fertile areas of opportunity come and go because information has become more widely accessible. I'm talking about whole countries where markets are great to trade. My edge is to constantly stay out in front of the curve. You forget that six or seven years ago investing in Thailand was considered pretty radical stuff. And now Thailand is mainstream. I'm on to Pakistan, or wherever. My edge is out there. I'm not afraid to identify it and then take my shot!

CHAPTER 18

Hard Times and Losin' It

Bryan Gindoff

Mr. Gindoff is a screenwriter residing in Los Angeles, California. Previously, he was president of Del Rey Investment Management.

Q: What first attracted you to trading?

Bryan: I grew up with it. My father was a CPA who had a real love for the stock market. We had a lot of dinner conversations about the stocks that he owned or the market in general. I suppose it was just in my bones.

He encouraged me to buy and sell shares and to do my research. So clearly the interest was planted at a young age. It was one of the things that I shared with my father in our relationship.

Q: Do you have any recollections that stand out that might have been important to you in your history as a trader?

Bryan: There was one particular trade that definitely had a lasting effect. My father was a very good investor in the Peter Lynch-Warren Buffett mold. He knew a lot about the companies he bought, he had a lot of conviction in them, and he liked to hold them forever. Sometime in the mid-60s, when I was still in school, I met a broker who kept his own charts and bought very fast-growing companies as the stocks broke out to new highs. At the time that was pretty radical stuff, but in the great bull market of the early 60s he had done phenomenally well.

Q: Back then stockbrokers with charts were held in about the same repute as fortune tellers and astrologers.

Bryan: Exactly. In truth, he was doing a lot of what William O'Neil codified for the general public years later. Anyhow, I was fascinated with the approach and I figured that I'd found something even better than my dad's stuffy old buy-'em-and-hold-'em ideas. So I took all my money and bought Syntex, which was one of the hottest stocks in the world at the time—they were the leading drug company making birth control pills. If I remember right, I bought the stock the day it touched 100 and the exact day the Dow hit 1,000 for the first time. It was a seminal experience for me. Here we were in the midst of this extraordinary bull market that ran from '62 to '66 and I absolutely top-ticked both the stock and the market that day.

A few weeks later the stock was down a lot and the market was down a lot and this was something that was totally outside of my previous experience. The truth is, I was absolutely oblivious to market risk. It was completely outside of any expectation I had ever had. I can remember when the stock got down to about 80 I was absolutely appalled and scared.

Q: Did you feel it was a personal affront?

Bryan: No. I don't think I took it that way. What I recollect was thinking how in the world could this happen to me? I never saw it coming! And I felt lousy and had the typical reaction, now that it has gone to 80, how much lower can it go? Also I better get out before I get destroyed. I sold the stock, took my loss, and in many ways it was an experience that really stayed with me. It was my first important lesson in risk control. It was a simple lesson that hey, stocks can go down! And it was a really critical lesson about having to know what your risk tolerance is before you ever enter the trade in the first place. Syntex ended up getting clobbered in the '66 bear market. As best as I can recollect, it never got back anywhere near its old highs. I've thought many times how incredibly lucky I was to have had this experience very early in my life.

Q: Bryan, your experience and background are really pretty unique. You've been a professional portfolio manager, handling fairly significant sums of investor capital as well as being a successful professional writer. You've written a number of screenplays that were made into fairly well-known movies. There was *Hard Times,* which starred . . .

Bryan: Charles Bronson, James Coburn, and Jill Ireland.

Q: Right. And you wrote Tom Cruise's first movie.

Bryan: I co-wrote both films. The one you're thinking of is Tom Cruise's first starring film, *Losin' It.* I was also one of the producers of *Losin' It.*

Q: Could you talk a little bit about your writing career and how it relates to trading?

Bryan: Well, I've always thought that I have this sort of bifurcated brain. On one side there's this interest in business and trading and on the other side there's an artist. Maybe that's a presumptuous thing to say. Other people have to call you an artist. But I think you know what I mean.

Q: Right brain–left brain sort of theory?

Bryan: Yeah—but unlike most people who are very heavily on one side or the other their whole life, my life tends to go back and forth like a pendulum between the two.

I went to UCLA and got a degree in economics but I also developed a real passion for movies. I went to every film festival that there was in Los Angeles and basically taught myself about writing and films because I never had the opportunity to go to film school. After I finished college I decided to pursue a career in film. I started knocking on doors in Hollywood trying to find a job. It was kind of frustrating at first because I wasn't very successful at getting a job so I started writing almost out of self-defense. Writing, like trading, is one of those things you can do for your own account. Nobody has to hire you. Of course, you hope that something good will come of it! So, I was writing and then I got fortunate enough to finally sell a screenplay.

Eventually I established myself and, as you know, I've had a fairly long run as a screenwriter in Hollywood. I wrote the pictures you mentioned before and, like most writers in Hollywood,

I ended up getting paid for an awful lot of screenplays that never found their way to the screen.

Q: You made a distinction between your artistic side and your business side. Obviously you were able to amalgamate the two in your film career.

Bryan: That's very true in the sense that, for a good part of my career in Hollywood, I've also been a producer. So it's a real amalgamation.

Q: Do you feel trading is similar in the sense that it requires both creative and analytical skills?

Bryan: I think for most traders that's true. Of course, there are certain individuals who are totally quantitative traders; basically they're mathematicians at heart. They develop their models and trade strictly off their computer. However, I think that tends to be a minority. So, if we kind of rule out that group, I think for most successful traders it is an integration of the two. I'll illustrate what I mean.

In both writing and in the stock market there is a common thread. The greatest success as a writer or as a trader comes from identifying a strong story or a strong theme. In Hollywood, it's said very often that if your story is strong enough, it will tend to transcend poor execution. There are many screenplays that are not particularly well written that have become very successful films but they have very compelling stories.

Q: And the success of the film is a result of the strength of the story.

Bryan: Right. The dialogue may not be that brilliant or the acting may be a little stiff. In general, the execution of the film may be fairly average. But if the story itself is strong, the film will make it.

Q: What would be an example of that kind of film?

Bryan: Well, this is both a book and film example, but I think that Tom Clancy's books, and the films that have been made from them, are pretty good examples. Clancy is a great storyteller. His basic story ideas are all exceptionally strong and his plotting is terrific. As they say, his books are real page-turners. But his characters, especially his lead character, Jack Ryan—they're really thin characters who aren't all that interesting and the dialogue isn't all that great. But because the story ideas are so strong, it doesn't matter. They succeed.

Q: Having Harrison Ford doesn't hurt either.

Bryan: That's actually a very astute observation. With a character as one-dimensional as Jack Ryan, you really need an extremely appealing and likable actor like Harrison Ford to make it all work on the screen. One of the problems with *The Hunt for Red October* was that it didn't star Harrison Ford, and yet, because the story's so strong, the film still succeeded.

Q: So if Tom Clancy goes public he's probably a pretty good investment, but how do you relate this story concept to the market?

Bryan: On Wall Street, just like in Hollywood, you want to look for a very strong story that's so powerful that it can succeed in spite of what might not be great execution, and if you can find great execution to go along with it, then you really hit the jackpot. For instance, in the last five years, one of the strongest stories has been computer networking stocks. About five years ago if you looked at the world and said, "Hey, there are all these zillions of computers out there and somehow they're all going to have to get tied together so they can communicate with each other," well, you had an incredibly strong story there.

So then if you went looking in the networking sector for stocks to buy, as opposed to other sectors of the market, you dramatically increased your probability of making a much higher return on your money. There's a good chance that you could have done quite well for awhile just buying a large basket of networking stocks, because the market was recognizing the strength of the basic idea and carrying poor to average companies along for the ride with the very good companies. You see that all the time in the market.

And if you went the next step and identified the leaders—Cisco, Cabletron, 3 Com, for instance, then you really did make tons of money. Essentially those were the companies that not only had the compelling story idea, but they also executed it with great dialogue and a great cast.

Q: What you're saying is that your life experiences in Hollywood and in the market have combined in a way that's led you to use very similar criteria in evaluating profit opportunity in both arenas?

Bryan: Yeah, in a broad sense, that's absolutely true. I think there really is a good analogy between how you make money in the movie business and how you make money in the market. Movie studios make their big money from blockbusters, which are often referred to as "tent-poles," the pictures that hold up the tent, so to speak. Generally, if you're going to have a shot at making outsized returns in a portfolio, you need a few tent-pole stocks—core holdings where you concentrate more of your money because you've found a company or a few companies with compelling stories, and, hopefully, great execution too. In both arenas I believe the biggest money is almost always made when you can tap into the compelling themes.

Q: Bryan, do you think trading is more of a learned skill or a natural talent?

Bryan: I think it's just like writing. I believe that you have to start with a certain aptitude. Some people just have a certain amount of natural writing talent. Who knows where it comes from? Once you have that talent, then you have to work very hard on perfecting your craft. I believe the same thing is true with trading. Some people have a natural aptitude and interest and then they work hard at perfecting their technique. I see a lot of similarity between writing and trading. Both require natural skills as well as learned behaviors and techniques. I think you made that point very well in *The Innergame of Trading.*

Q: I'll make sure that last sentence makes it through the final edit.

Bryan: I mean, your point in the book kind of crosses over to both of my careers. Ultimately, success in either derives from knowing yourself. As a trader it comes from getting yourself in sync with the market and who you are, on a fairly profound psychological level. I think the same thing is obviously true about writing. Your best writing is always when you're writing from the heart, when your story is truly coming out of you.

I think the same thing happens in trading. There's an expression often used in sports—I think it's now starting to kind of permeate our language. People talk about getting "in the zone." You see it a lot in sports where an athlete just seems to be in the zone. They can't miss, right?

Q: It's like Michael Jordan during the playoffs sinking six three-pointers. His concentration is so intense yet he looks completely relaxed!

Bryan: Coming from Los Angeles I would say it was more like Magic Johnson against the Celtics a few years earlier. You see a great athlete in that state longing for the ball with two seconds left on the clock. They know and you know it's going to go in. He's not going to miss! And yet we all know that their ability to come through in the clutch comes from combining the natural talent with all those thousands of hours of practice, from taking that shot over and over and over again. I have certainly experienced that in trading so I know the same thing happens. You've done all your homework. You've been watching the market. The stock sets up just as you had anticipated. You execute the trade and watch it unfold in front of you, exactly as planned. It's as if the world goes into slow motion for a moment, which, I suspect, is what it feels like when you're on the basketball court.

Q: And you're just in that moment of time . . .

Bryan: Only in that moment! And instead of feeling uptight, you're feeling very relaxed and you simply execute. You don't think about the hundred thousand little moves that it takes to put the ball in the basket, you just do it!

Q: As a writer, and as a trader, how do you get in the zone?

Bryan: You have to get in sync with yourself, which I think is your basic point. Whatever you're writing or whatever you're trading, it's not an artificial thing outside yourself. The motivation is coming from your deepest convictions. That's one of the conditions that makes for very good writing and very good trading. Beyond that, though, I think there are some other similarities. In both cases, you genuinely need to have done your homework. I think you can only get in the zone when you've already done your homework so that when the situation presents itself, you're then able to act. When you haven't done your homework, you're lost. When you haven't prepared, your intuition doesn't get you anywhere. Or maybe what happens is a lot of negative stuff just takes over.

Q: My view is a simple one: The intuition is just the dividend for all the hard work.

Bryan: It's like the Thomas Edison quote. "Genius is 99 percent perspiration and 1 percent inspiration."

Q: My favorite Edison quote actually makes the same point. He said, "Most people don't recognize opportunity because it goes around disguising itself as hard work wearing overalls."

Bryan: I had never heard that before. It's brilliant. I think what happens in both writing and trading is that you have to do a lot of hard work. And, if you do, you can have those wonderful moments where you get on this extreme high, where instinctively you just do the right thing. As a writer, the words literally start flowing out of you because you've gone through all the preparation and perspiration.

I don't think it's possible for a trader to be in that zone all the time any more than I think it is for a writer. I think what happens in both writing and trading is that as you get more confident you're able to visit that state of mind more often. That's the best answer I can give you. I know for me the key is to always work hard at knowing myself.

Q: What has trading taught you about yourself?

Bryan: I think trading has taught me a lot. As a matter of fact, I think the whole process, if you allow yourself to really be open, is like going through psychotherapy every day. It really gives you an opportunity to see what you're all about.

Q: I would say it's like psychotherapy, except it's tough!

Bryan: I suppose that's absolutely true. The market forces you, if you're going to succeed, to be completely honest with yourself. If you're losing money, you are simply forced to confront that reality. It's an objective reality, it's right in front of you and you have to acknowledge it. Truthfully, I believe the market weeds out people who are unable to be honest with themselves. I suspect that trading, aside from being a fascinating way to make a living, is also one of the most self-revelatory things that a person can do. Day in and day out you're confronted with all these primal emotions. You're in the market, it's going drastically against you, and you have to deal with that fight-or-flight reflex.

Q: And it's all about how you respond!

Bryan: There are very few occupations in which a human being has to confront inner emotions as regularly as a trader does. If you can't be honest about acknowledging what you're feeling, you're on a sure path to destruction.

Q: What do you think distinguishes you from all the other traders?

Bryan: That's a good question. I guess I would also ask myself what makes me a different writer from all the other writers out there? The answer is I have my own voice. It's something that I've learned to project and identify as truly my own.

A voice is a very subjective thing. It's your individual style or way of telling a story that you have developed over time as a result of a lot of soul searching and hard work. I think as a trader, the same thing applies. If you've been able to create a voice as a trader, that's your individual approach and method of identifying opportunity. Whether a writer or a trader, your voice is what is uniquely you.

CHAPTER 19

Momma Said There'd Be Days Like This

Angelo Reynolds

Mr. Reynolds is a member of the International Monetary Market, where he trades his own account. He specializes in the Eurodollar contract.

Q: What first attracted you to trading?

Angelo: I was a sophomore at Wharton and a friend of mine from California received a birthday present in the mail, 10,000 shares of IBM. I started following IBM and watched it skyrocket! From that point on I decided that I wanted to be involved in the market.

Q: Why did you want to get involved?

Angelo: I thought trading really kind of suited my abilities. I've always been very quick with numbers and liked to make money. I knew from an early age that I would have a lot of money. I felt trading was one of the few professions where people could go from not having anything to becoming millionaires. You can get a legitimate shot. Unless you're in athletics or the movie or music industry, you don't get that kind of opportunity.

Q: Where did you grow up?

Angelo: West Philadelphia. My mother was a school teacher and I had six sisters.

Q: And you were the only boy in the family?

Angelo: Yes.

Q: Those are rough odds!

Angelo: Yeah, especially since my dad died when I was in the second grade.

Q: You said you always knew that you were going to have a lot of money. Where did that come from?

Angelo: I've always thought I was above average in intelligence and, from an early age, my academic performance kind of confirmed that. I guess you would have to say I've always been confident, not only in academics but just confident as a person. I've always felt, in some sense, that I was gifted. God gave me certain talent, perhaps to show other people that they could succeed in whatever field they chose. And I've thought I always had something to prove. I think it was because I wanted to look out for my mom after my dad died. There was no other man there, it was just me! I told her one day I was going to make a lot of money and take care of her. That has always been a tremendous motivation for me.

Q: Do you think there's anything in your background that prepared you for trading?

Angelo: As you know, there are a lot of ex-athletes down on the trading floor and they tend to be very successful. Sports has been a big part of my life and I think it's great preparation for an arena like trading. The fact that you discipline yourself to practice hard every day, learning to deal with victory and defeat, always giving your best effort. In trading if you play your best game, whether you make money that day or not, you can always feel proud of yourself.

Q: What sports did you play?

Angelo: I ran cross-country in high school and played basketball from grade school throughout college.

Q: You played college ball?

Angelo: Yes.

Q: What position did you play?

Angelo: Shooting guard, emphasis on the shooting.

Q: So, you know how to handle the ball and you like to shoot!

Angelo: Yeah, I love to play. I've always loved to play basketball and I was pretty good.

Q: Do you see any similarities between being a shooting guard and trading on the exchange floor?

Angelo: Especially being a shooting guard, because you take a lot of shots! In the pit, you have to take shots: in other words, you have to look for opportunities where you think you can score. But for me I think the analogy is wider now; I think it encompasses all of athletics. Trading requires the same thing that you need in athletics, discipline. To be a successful athlete, there is mental preparation that you have to do before the game. You have to prepare and concentrate; you have to see yourself doing positive things on the court or in the field. You just have to be prepared to go out there and be a player.

Q: Angelo, how did you actually get started in the market?

Angelo: A friend of mine I played with in high school got a job right out of school on the trading floor working for First Options.

Q: Which trading floor?

Angelo: The Philadelphia Stock Exchange. We were really close. I went to talk to him one day. I was trying to decide what I was going to do. He suggested I come down to the trading floor and give it a shot. So I started working as a runner in the stock options in 1984; I worked for a firm out of Chicago. We had a pretty good options team. Our manager always stressed the fundamentals and the basics in the business.

Q: What fundamentals?

Angelo: He said never make any assumptions. For instance, if I was working a phone order, I was to always double- or triple-check every detail, because it's a business that revolves around details. It's easy to make mistakes. How many times when taking an order do people confuse 50 for 15? Those errors are made a million times over.

Q: So you were really focused on the details and the mechanics of trading?

Angelo: Yes. I worked there for about a year. I really liked the atmosphere and the people.

Q: Were you doing any trading or strictly handling clients?

Angelo: At this point, I was just getting my feet wet. I pretty much did everything! I answered retail phones for six months, then moved up to handling institutional and proprietary traders. Traders for Solly, Morgan and other institutions.

At the same time, I started doing a lot of reading. The more I read about the markets, the more I realized I wanted a career in trading. By now, my desire to be a trader was pretty strong! I got a job filling orders in the currency options in 1986, and that moved me to another level.

A lot of stocks were getting taken over, so Philadelphia kept losing stock listings. But there was a lot of business going on in the currency options. It turned out to be a big market for the exchange.

Q: And you were filling in the currency options.

Angelo: Yes.

Q: Doing any trading yet?

Angelo: No.

Q: But you wanted to?

Angelo: Yes, of course I did. I was still primarily trading for clients and the more orders I filled, the more I wanted to trade for my own account. I didn't actually trade for myself until I came to Chicago. I left Philadelphia in 1991. The market there just dried up. I was offered a job by two large locals in Chicago to be part of their trading group. They were spreaders in the Eurodollars. Unfortunately, my part was still primarily filling orders rather then trading. It wasn't until 1994 that I was given the opportunity to trade on the Eurodollars from another Chicago market maker who ran his own proprietary trading group. And I've got to tell you at this point it was really important for me to get to trade so that I could realize my goal.

Q: Which goal?

Angelo: To make $1 million and buy a nice house for my mother! I can remember exactly the way I felt on my first day of trading. It was scary! I told myself that I'd waited a long time for this opportunity and I'd make the most of it. I was going to give it my best shot and not sit back and play it safe. I wasn't going to allow myself to be controlled by my fears.

Q: What was your biggest fear?

Angelo: I've never spoken about this but maybe that I wouldn't be good enough. I mean, it takes a lot to be able to get the edge in these markets. You can't trade small size and expect the edge. You've got to be trading at least 50 contracts or more. That means you're risking at least $1,250 a tick and usually more. Another fear was that as a broker you have a guaranteed income! If you suck as a trader, you're going to be out the door! I would say that that was my biggest fear.

Q: And of course, you wouldn't be able to buy your mom her new house!

Angelo: Right. I learned a long time ago in sports there is a world of difference between thinking and doing. I was afraid and I think it was a natural fear. I mean I was going against some of the best traders in the world! But in no way did I ever believe that I wasn't going to succeed like I had in everything else I ever did in my life.

Q: So what actually happened on that first day?

Angelo: The first trade I made I bought ten contracts. The market immediately went in my direction and I made $250. It was an exhilarating feeling!

I was really feeling good and didn't see a lot to do in the market until later in the session. And there it was! I saw something that I thought could really pay off and was committed to play to win. So I stepped out and bought a 100 contracts and I was right again! At the end of the day I had made $5,000. I got home and my wife greeted me at the door. All I said was, "Honey, we're going to be rich."

Q: That kind of performance can go a long way in helping you overcome the initial fears you had mentioned!

Angelo: It was one of the best feelings I have ever experienced in my life. I felt I was put to the test and proved my mettle. You really never know how people are going to perform in high pressure situations until they're placed under fire. I have seen guys on the trading floor with Harvard degrees not make it and others right off the street who've proven themselves brilliantly. Some guys just get in the pit and freeze up. Other guys can't tolerate the uncertainty.

Success has a lot to do with personality factors. Your mental toughness and desire to win and your appetite for risk. Some people just want to buy something that has an FDIC guarantee on it or a promised return. There are a lot of different things that go into being a successful trader, and more of them are psychological. After my first day I was able to overcome my initial apprehension and knew I could do it. I knew I had the courage.

Q: What do you mean by courage?

Angelo: I'll give you an example. A week after I was in the pit, I was bidding for the market at a particular price along with four other locals. This broker, I think, had it in for me, maybe because I was new, or I trade aggressively, who knows. He had a large order to sell and the way he divided it up, I just knew he was trying to stuff me! He gave 50 contracts to each of the other market makers and hit me with 300. I could have said to him at that point, "No, 50 only!" but I wouldn't give him that satisfaction!

Q: Do you think he was trying to test you or show you up in front of the other traders?

Angelo: Sure he was!

Q: He was playing a game with you!

Angelo: He wanted me to blink, to back down and look like an idiot in front of the other traders in the pit. It took courage because first of all, I had to justify to myself that at $7,500 a tick it was the right trade to make and that I could handle it whether or not that particular broker hit me. And also to make it clear to him that I would not allow him to exert control. As a result of that experience I got an incredible amount of respect from the other brokers around the pit. They respected my trading and my refusal to be manipulated. I guess that's just one instance!

Q: Angelo, you speak very persuasively about courage and how you have expressed it in your trading. You are the only African-American trading in the Eurodollar pit. What has that experience been like?

Angelo: It's just one more thing that you have to deal with if you want to be successful. I've always been told and certainly try to live my life in a way that I judge people on their talent and their character. If somebody shows me that they're biased, or that they're not worthy of my friendship or admiration, I'll treat them accordingly. We all like to be judged on our merits. One thing I'm sure of, if I'm judged on those qualities, people couldn't have anything but good things to say about me!

But let's face it—people do have certain stereotypes. Depending on where they come from, they may not have ever known a black person. Of course, I realize that there are situations when these things happen and I deal with them. One thing I will tell you: I will always try to be fair about it and, by the same token, if someone has a stereotype that I'm not really happy with, I'll let them know.

Q: Have there been any incidents that come to mind?

Angelo: Occasionally, someone will make a comment to be comical that I might not find particularly funny, and I'll tell him. I might tell him that someone who is as intelligent as him can come up with something better than that. That usually shuts him up!

Q: Of course, the trading pit is also the biggest locker room in the world! People say things there that are so adolescent it's really amazing.

Angelo: If it comes down to a dispute over a trade, or who did what to whom, that's one thing. If it's not racial, usually there's a right and wrong to any situation. If I do something wrong, and I'm aware of it, I'm the first one to admit it and say, "Hey, I screwed up!" Or if someone else does something wrong, I have no problem saying, "Look, that's wrong."

The bottom line is I have to stand up for myself, because there's nobody else there who's going to do it. When people get into arguments they say all kinds of things, particularly on the floor. You have to stand up for yourself, because once somebody knows they can roll over you, they're just going to eat you for lunch!

Q: It can be a rather cannibalistic atmosphere.

Angelo: Look, please understand I will go off more than anybody else. I mean, I've had times when I just totally blow up, but that's usually because I think I'm right. It's got nothing to do with someone's personality or their ethnic background. I never used that as a diving board to start an argument. There are enough disputes that have to be resolved on the floor based on who was right or wrong in a particular situation relying on the facts and the issues without all the personal stuff. I guess what it comes down to is I'm really not afraid of anybody down there.

Q: Not afraid in what sense?

Angelo: Well, physically, mentally. I've gotten into some very intimidating confrontations because, as I said before, I came into the pit trading size; after a couple of weeks I was a 300-lot trader. I was getting trades and the other big traders were accusing me of stealing "their" trades.

Q: How'd you handle these confrontations?

Angelo: There was one trader in particular who could be very intimidating. I told him, "Look, you might scare the rest of these guys, but you don't scare me!" This guy was supposed to be like a fifth-degree something or other in martial arts and everybody was afraid of him. When he would come in the pit he would shadowbox to show people that he had karate skills and he could fight. He just had a reputation of being a tough guy and, on top of that, he was a very big trader. So people were just naturally intimidated by him. He would trade 500 or 1,000 at a clip and treated the other locals shamelessly and none of them would ever say anything to him. About a month after I arrived in the pit, I bought 300 contracts from one of the brokers at a time when this trader was heavily short. Apparently, he didn't like that and he started calling me all kinds of names. I just let him know right then and there that he could talk all he wanted but he wasn't going to intimidate me. I said to him, "Hey, there is just air between me and you. If you want to do something, I'm right here; have a piece of me." I'm from West Philadelphia. Believe me, there were a lot of tough guys where I came from!

I think that fear is something that everybody deals with, even the greatest athletes. I was watching an interview with Mike Tyson. He was talking about a fight that he had when he was a teenager. Before the fight he was petrified. He was scared shitless! But once he got in the ring he wound up knocking out his opponent in 17 seconds! His manager told him something that I have found to be true and very useful. It is very simple: Everybody's afraid. It's what you do with that fear that separates the guy who is a coward from the guy who is courageous. Personally, I would rather give it my best shot and fail than to look back and say I didn't have the courage to really "be there" in trading and everything else.

Q: What has trading taught you about yourself?

Angelo: It taught me that the discipline that my mother instilled in me at an early age is really very beneficial, and that I should never lose focus of what I want to accomplish because the moment I stray it costs me financially and emotionally.

Q: Financially and emotionally?

Angelo: And morally. My mother always taught me to be strong. Trading has allowed me to become a strong person, because I've gone through a lot of ups and downs. I think the early part was the most instructive for me; getting through the first six months or the first year. I've learned that I've got a lot of good characteristics, and if I continue to work hard I'll reach all the goals that I've set for myself.

Q: What distinguishes Angelo Reynolds from all the other traders?

Angelo: What makes me unique? The easy answer, of course, is being an African-American. Sometimes I feel like I'm under a microscope. I've always wanted to represent myself and my family and my race well. Other things that make me unique: I think I have more confidence than most traders because I don't know of too many traders who came onto the floor and immediately became players trading the size that I do. My commitment to developing my skills I believe is also unique. I just keep myself constantly growing both in terms of skills and my capital base.

Another thing that makes me unique is that I had to overcome a lot in my life. My dad died when I was seven, I didn't have any male guidance in my family. I went from living at home to going to live in private boarding school.

I think this has made me stronger as a person. I think that growing up in the neighborhood that I come from and experiencing some of the things that I did as a kid, well, that's why my mom wanted to get me off the street, away from the gangs in the neighborhood. She put me in a private school after my dad died. I was one of the first black students to go to this particular school, and you couldn't come home to see your family except for holidays. Being taken out of my neighborhood, away from family and friends and then being placed in this school, it was totally foreign to me. I cried for a month. But you know what happened? I ended up making some of the best friends that I ever had in my life. I was exposed to things that were totally outside my world.

Q: Does trading on the floor ever feel like that boarding school?

Angelo: Well, when I walked in to the trading pit on that first day, it did. I was afraid and kind of intimidated, but after six months it felt like my best friend.

Life doesn't always work out to be the way you draw it up on a chalkboard. And like every other trader, I have my ups and downs, but so far, it's been okay!

CHAPTER 20

Futures and Options

"In the middle of difficulty lies opportunity."
—Albert Einstein

"Man is not free to refuse to do the thing which gives him more pleasure than any other conceivable action."
—Stendahl

The true winning skills of the trader, whether operating on the floor or managing a billion-dollar portfolio, are psychological rather than tactical or strategic in nature. When asked what is a successful trader, Leo Melamed responded, "There is much to being a successful trader. There are many rules to be applied and many lessons to be learned. There must be a willingness and ability to learn to comprehend fundamentals and statistics, to grasp technical application, to develop an inner trading sense, to accept defeat and live with victory and much more. But most of all, there must be present a multitude of inborn characteristics relating to the trader's personality, psychology, emotional equilibrium, courage and patience."

In the final analysis, I believe it all comes down to this: discipline, focus, optimism, and confidence.

Discipline

Discipline is a purely psychological characteristic. For some it is inborn, but for most traders it is acquired along the way. It is literally the ability to refocus attention at the moment of decision away from one's normal fears and associations. It is the mental skill to overcome the trader's natural need for control and certainty (which can never be had) and a basic aversion to pain (taking losses). It is teaching oneself to visualize, hear, and feel imagery and associations that enhance trading performance. In addition, it is internalizing a belief system that assumes a successful trading result.

Pat Arbor, chairman of the board of the Chicago Board of Trade, had this to say: "The essential characteristic required for successful trading, bottom-line, comes down to one thing, discipline. Discipline is the way you handle yourself no matter what else is going on around you. Having it results in success. Lacking discipline, you're a loser."

Jack Sandner, chairman of the board of the Chicago Mercantile Exchange added this: "Discipline means many different things to people, but I think its main ingredient is focus. They say traders have a nice life. They come in at 8:30 and they're gone at 1:00. You see their expensive cars going down the expressway! What people don't realize is that a lot happens before the bell rings and a lot happens after the bell rings. The other thing people don't realize is between the opening and closing bell a tremendous energy is expended in focus, if you're any good at what you do. I don't know one trader that's any good that doesn't really focus 1,000 percent every second on what he's doing, and is consumed by it! And the traders that don't are lazy; they'll make money sometimes, but eventually they'll get caught. I think it takes a tremendous attention span and focus. If you don't, then the discipline can't follow. You can't be disciplined unless you focus, because it's too easy to look away and rationalize."

Focus

As I pointed out in *The Intuitive Trader* (Wiley, 1996) there is an optimum performance state for the trader that is characterized by the following: physical, relaxation, psychological calm, a feeling of positive expectation, energized demeanor, active engagement, alertness, effortlessness, anxiety management, and being in control. It is in fact a unified experience of heightened focus, where the trader feels totally, and realistically, confident and automatic in his or her response.

Traders who have experienced this level of focus often refer to it as being in "the zone." They report feeling relaxed and loose; an inner quiet and calmness; intensity; and having fun and letting go.

Donald Sliter, one of the largest independent floor traders of the S&P 500, had this to say: "I'll tell you what; I get in a zone. I'll trade thousands of S&P contracts in a day, and I'm just moving in and moving out, feeling great, eating up everything in sight. I get in the car in the morning and I'm juiced. I can't wait, especially on number days or on expirations. I get so pumped up sometimes—just the idea that each day is going to be different, that I'm in control of my own situation, my own destiny, every single day. There's nobody to answer to. Everything you do you're either rewarded or spanked for."

Linda Leventhal, arguably the most successful trader on the International Monetary Market, put it this way: "When you're in the trading pit, I would say it's very much like being in a race or a prize fight or for that matter on the stage. You're performing! You are performing all the time. And if you're not paying full attention, you will get caught. You may have been out too late or maybe you partied too much or whatever. You allow yourself to become distracted. You can lose everything in one momentary lapse. Being focused is really being there!"

Optimism

Optimism is being constantly in a state of mind that allows the trader to have a positive expectation about himself and market opportunities. It is only as a result of the trader adopting a system of empowering personal thoughts, beliefs, and attitudes that well-analyzed trades and market opportunities can be automatically and effortlessly executed.

Bruce Johnson, president of Packers Trading, had this to say about the role of optimism: "I always say to myself in the morning I'm going to have a good day. And even if it isn't good, I always kind of look on the bright side of everything. I'm really the eternal optimist, which I think is essential. I mean it's the key ingredient in being a good trader! You just have to stay positive."

Consider the beliefs expressed by the top-performing traders about themselves and the market:

- I believe I'm a successful trader.
- I believe I can consistently achieve excellent results.
- I believe I can identify winning trades.
- I believe I am confident.
- I believe each day's performance is fresh.
- I believe I've got what it takes
- I believe I can be successful without being perfect.
- I believe I can take a series of losses and still have a successful result.
- I believe the market offers limitless opportunities.

An essential aspect of optimism is a willingness and commitment to continuously strive to improve. Jeffery Silverman summed it up this way in *The Innergame of Trading:* "You must be willing to work hard and know yourself. You must spend the time. You must study the characteristics of successful traders. You must study your own mistakes. You must study the mistakes of the others around you. Increasing levels of sophistication will put you in the direction of understanding who you are."

From *The Intuitive Trader:* "Trading contains much of the comedy and drama of life. In many ways it is a microcosm of life. There is joy, uncertainty, frustration, pain, and struggle. The ultimate test in trading is always to accept the gauntlet of the ultimate challenge: self-control and self-mastery. It is a continuous process, a transformative process, where the trader can change and be born anew. It involves courage, optimism, and the discipline to succeed and the intuition that trading does not have to be a score-card of self-evaluation when it can be a 360-degree universe of self-realization. The challenge is ours. It is a contest of each trader against oneself. Right now, physically calm, mentally relaxed in the moment."

Confidence

Confidence is the trader's ultimate bet on his or her own abilities. It is the profound belief in self that Tim McAuliffe expressed when he said with three seconds left on the shot clock he wants the basketball. He is not going to pass it off or hesitate, because in a real sense as a basketball player or as a trader, he believes no one in the world in this instant can do a better job!

Jack Sandner expressed the importance of confidence this way: "You have to have a tremendous confidence in yourself and your ability, and that trading is a cycle like everything else is a cycle, and at the end of the term it will turn your way if you have confidence in yourself and do all the right things."

* * * * *

The traders who have learned the importance of discipline, focus, optimism, and confidence come in all colors, shapes, and sizes; across far-reaching borders, internal and beyond; armed with sophisticated degrees and certificates and, in some cases, no formal certification at all.

In the trading theater, they perform a powerful financial pageant in which new players act out age-old desires: the search for treasure in button-down shirts and Nike sneakers. Sweaty, loud, combative postadolescents, at times heedless of consequences, are engaged in a constant crusade to make money and to spend it on every kind of imaginable extravagance. The actors are men and women mostly in their 20s and 30s, inhabiting a feverish, sex-charged world of gestures and dollar worship. The trading floor is a blue-collar atmosphere with custom white-collar rewards, a universe of expectation and promise where lives can be changed forever in a Chicago instant.

The trading theater is at one and the same time a vulgar capitalistic vision of wasted resources and ambition and the ideal and epitome of what everybody wants. It is an electrified world of unlimited possibility and gold fever; a dream factory with elaborate stage sets and stuntmen. Like members of the Starship Enterprise, these men and women are committed with unwavering devotion to their ultimate quest.

Their mission is as historic and immediate as the American dream. It is an exaggerated, perhaps bastardized, dream and yet it is as true and pure as the American dream itself: talented, hardworking individuals possessing a vision, locked in a perpetual struggle one on one with themselves.

I have tried to enter the complex and yet subtle world of the trader's psyche in a way that is both down-to-earth and far-reaching. It has been my objective to allow each trader to relate an adventure story of his or her own experience rather than offer a sermon or lecture. I have tried to accomplish this with great respect and affection for my fellow traders: clear-eyed, free of sentimentality, cant, or theory.

INDEX

A

Abstract structure, 45–46
Adaptation, 80
Advancers, 107
Analysis, market profile, 108–9, 114
Analytical approach, 17–18, 22
Annie Hall, 54
Ansani, Mike, 165
Arbor, Patrick, 4–5, 199
Art, trading as, 83
Austrian perspective, of
    economics, 116

B

Barnes, Rickey, 60
Baruch, Bernard, 36
Basketball analogies, 185–90
Bear market, 90
Big Player, The, 129
Blackjack, 129–30
Blockbuster Video, 89
Bond options, 140–41
Brandywine Asset Management, 16
Brennan, Tim, 69
Brodsky, Bill, 13
Bull market, 80–81
Busch, Arlene, 139–48

C

Campaign trading, 125
Camus, 108
Cashman, Gene, 59
Cattle market, 125
Challenge, 18–19
Chicago Mercantile Exchange,
    chairman of, 8
CK Partners, Inc., 33
Cohen, Solomon, 33–46
    global perspective of, 42–43
    greatest strength as trader, 41

*Commodity Market Money
    Management,* 27
Commonwealth United, 88
Competitive spirit, 9–10, 48
Complacency, 28
Computer networking stocks, 183
Confidence, 71, 202
Control, 112–13
Coquest, Inc., 75
Correction, market, 90
Correlations, 123
Courage, 104, 193, 195–96
Crabel, William H. "Toby," 68–74
    greatest strength as trader, 72
Crash of 1987, 27, 40, 79–80, 155
Cresvale International
    Management, 139, 141

D

*Day Trading with Short-Term
    Price Patterns and Opening
    Range Breakout,* 68, 70
Dennis, Richard, 131–32, 133–34
Dever, Mike, 16–32, 132
    greatest strength as trader, 22
    trading systems, 23
Diamond, Barbara, 145
Diamond, Joe, 57–58
Discipline, 48, 49–50, 55, 61, 90,
    144, 151, 164, 176, 190, 196, 199
Drawdowns, 135, 138
Drummond, Charlie, 107–8, 113
Drummond geometry, 106–7

E

Eckhardt, Bill, 132, 133
Edison, Thomas, 186
Ego, 31, 61, 147
Einstein, Albert, 198
Eliot, T. S., 7

Eurodollar contracts, 191
European Rate Mechanism crisis, 147
Experience, 19

F

Fear, 10–11, 177, 195
Fight analogy, 79
First Option, 145
Flexibility, 172
Focus, 48, 200
Foster, Scott A., 116–28
    background preparation for trading, 121–22, 127–28
    greatest strength as trader, 124
    psychological approach, 127
Friedman, Ray, 99
Futures commission merchant, 98

G

Gambling, 169
Game playing, 17
Gazelle Global Fund Limited, 33, 37
Gehm, Fred, 27
Gindoff, Bryan, 179–87
    screenwriting career, 181–82
Girard, Doug, 153
Gordon, David M., 87–95
    greatest strength as trader, 90
    loss of eyesight, 91–92
Grossman, Tom, 167–78
    background preparation for trading, 168–69, 176–77
    greatest strength as trader, 172

H

Hawksbill Capital Management, 129
Hedge fund industry, 37–38
Heron, David, 39–40
Hierarchy of Needs, The, 12
Hippocrates, 95
Hull, Blair, 131
Hull Trading Company, 131
Humility, 90
Hunt fiasco, 11

I

Ice ball theory, 31–32
Independence, of mind, 26
Inefficiency in markets, identifying, 123–24
Information, processing of, 24
Innergame of Trading, The, 13, 36, 184
Integrity, 156
Intellectual challenge, of trading, 70
Intuition, 19, 35, 39
Intuitive Trader, The, 7, 142, 171, 201

J

James Capel, 141
Johnson, Bruce, 201
Johnson, Eddie, 58
Jones, Paul Tudor, 71

K

Kamen Stein & Associates, 98
Karma approach, 170
Kingdon Capital, 170

L

Lake Shore Asset Management, 56
Lansburgh, David, 157–66
    background preparation for trading, 158, 160–61
    greatest strength as trader, 162–63
Learned skills vs. talent, in trading, 38–39, 51, 71–72, 83, 89, 144, 161, 184
Learning and adapting, 80
Letterman, Jerry, 149–56
    background preparation for trading, 151
Leventhal, Linda, 6–7, 200
Leveraging, 120
Liffe Exchange, 141
Lind, Barry, 149
London, England, 33–34
Loss, response to, 10–11, 20–22, 27

M

McAuliffe, Timothy, 47–55, 177, 178, 202
   greatest strength as trader, 53
   background preparation for trading, 50
McGraw, Tug, 31
Maduff, Kamen and Stein, 103
Maduff, Sydney, 103–4
Magic analogy, 121–22
Market
   correction in, 90
   inefficiency in, identifying, 123–24
   profile, 108–9
Market Wizards, 88
Markham, Mark, 159–60
Maslow, Abraham, 12
Melamed, Leo, 6, 63, 198
Mental preparation, 190
Mesch, Robin, 106–15
   background preparation for trading, 111
   greatest strength as trader, 113
Moral code, 55
Motivation, 3
Movie analogy,184

N

Networking stocks, 183
Nicklaus, Jack, 83
Nin, Anaïs, 1

O

O'Neil, William, 180
Objectivity, 22, 31
Opening range system, 160
Optimism, 108, 201–2

P

Packers Trading, 201
Pattern recognition, 111
Personality, of trader, 86
Processing, of information, 24
Proprietary trading, 37–38
Psychology of individual, and trading, 133

R

"Rabbit theory," 88
Rafferty, Jerry, 76–77
Rand Financial Services, 96
Refco, 99, 139, 141–42
Respect, for markets, 85
Reynolds, Angelo, 188–97
   background preparation for trading, 189–90
Riffel, Adam, 61–62
Risk
   floor traders and, 154
   management of, 71
   /reward ratio, 50
Rosenberg, Larry, 56–67
   greatest strength as trader, 61
   background preparation for trading, 59

S

SAC International Equities, LLC, 167
Sandner, Jack, 5–6, 8–15, 199, 202
   background preparation for trading, 9–10
Scheinberg, Eric, 173–74
Schipani, Frank, 129
Screenwriting analogy, 183
Self-control, 202
Seykota, Ed, 88
Shanks, A. Thomas, 129–38
   background preparation for trading, 132
   greatest strength as trader, 134–35
Shatkin, Hank, 60
Shobin, Steve, 89
Silverman, Jeffrey, 36, 201
Sisyphus, 108
Sliter, Donald, 146, 200
Sports analogies, 161, 185, 190
Stein, Marshall, 96–105
   background preparation for trading, 96–97
Stendahl, 198
Stern, Lee, 56–57, 60
Stops, 90, 113
Stutemeyer, Pete, 113

Syntex, 180
System, for trading, 23
Systematic approach, 123

T

Taft, 130
Talent vs. training, 38–39, 51, 71
Technical analysis, 80
Thomson Research, 106
Trade structure, 113
Trading, as art form, 83
Trading Prophets—CBT Bonds, 106
Trading system, 23
Training vs. talent, 38–39, 51, 71
Turtles, 129, 131–33
Tyson, Mike, 195

U–V

Uston, Ken, 129
Volatility, 39, 70

W–Z

Wall Street Journal, 98
Weinmann, Dennis, 75–86
    background preparation for
        trading, 78–79, 82
    fight analogy, 79
    greatest strength as trader, 81
Winning, as protracted experience,
    10–13
Woods, Tiger, 83
Zone, 185–86, 200. *See also* Focus

About the Author

Robert Koppel is president of the Innergame Division of Rand Financial Services, Inc., a Chicago-based FCM clearing all major world exchanges. He is author of *The Intuitive Trader* (Wiley, 1996) and coauthor with Howard Abell of *The Innergame of Trading* (Irwin, 1993) and *The Outer Game of Trading* (Irwin, 1994). He is a former long-term member of the Chicago Mercantile Exchange. He holds advanced degrees in philosophy and group behavior from Columbia University. For more information, please contact:

Innergame Division
Rand Financial Services
30 South Wacker Drive, Suite 2200
Chicago, IL 60606
800-726-3088
http://www.innergame.com